HOMAGE TO GEORGE BARKER

on his sixtieth birthday

HOMAGE TO
GEORGE BARKER

ON HIS SIXTIETH BIRTHDAY

Edited by John Heath-Stubbs
and Martin Green

MARTIN BRIAN
& O'KEEFFE
London

First published in 1973
by Martin Brian & O'Keeffe Ltd
37 Museum Street London WC1

ISBN 0 85616 120 9
(Trade edition)

ISBN 0 85616 200 0
(Limited edition)

Printed in Great Britain
by W & J Mackay Limited, Chatham

Contents

Frontispiece portrait by Patrick Swift

Editorial Note	*page*	7
G. S. FRASER		9
PAUL POTTS		11
JOHN FULLER		21
THOMAS BLACKBURN		22
DAVID GASCOYNE		23
ALLEN GINSBERG		25
BERNARD SAINT		26
DAVID WRIGHT		29
JAMES LIDDY		36
PAUL DURCAN		39
JOHN HEATH-STUBBS		40
MAURICE CARPENTER		41
GEOFFREY HILL		46
MARTIN GREEN		48
KARL MILLER		50
PETER LEVI		55
PATRICK SWIFT		57
OLIVER BERNARD		76
ANTHONY THWAITE		78
C. H. SISSON		83
Bibliography		89

Editorial Note

The editors in bringing this book together don't pretend that the contributors necessarily represent all of George Barker's friends or admirers who should or could have been included. One or two who were originally approached made no reply; others apologized owing to pressure of work.

They would like to thank firstly the contributors and secondly to make acknowledgements to the *New Statesman* for permission to reproduce Karl Miller's review, 'Infidelity', and to the Oxford University Press for permission to reprint 'The Sacred Hearth' from *David Gascoyne: Collected Poems.*

To George Barker, for his Sixtieth Birthday

G. S. FRASER

Flash Harry, I used to call you,
The man for the three-card trick,
The thimble-rigger, the con man
With a loverly golden brick,

The cap with perhaps a razor-skip,
The scarf, the moll called Elsie,*
Holding hunched court in a Fulham pub
Not in my snobby Chelsea,

One for a 1930's movie:
Legs Diamonds Rises and Falls.
Do you write 'poems' or 'poetry'?
(Nobody doubts you have balls.)

Legs and diamonds are just the thing,
The verse dances and glitters.
But total structure of short poem—
Send it back to the fitters?

Gaudy and glittering verses
For a fair-ground Pearly King,
A Barker? (But role rehearses
Soul, which is everything.)

* *Elsie:* this female Christian name is brought in for convenience
of rhyme only. There was no such person. G. S. F.

Big bully-boys can be kind.
In a Fleet Street pub you pled:
'Sorry, you write like an angel on Yeats!'
'I rise with my subject,' I said.

Little I've seen of you since.
You have had women and fame.
Which matters more, which less?
Neither perhaps? the game?

Men get what they imagine.
I imagined suburban peace
And loving students. I think that you
Imagined guilt and release

And lately when I have met you
Your bliss of release is bland:
Still raffish and gallant at sixty
Shyly kind, and informally grand.

Men sometimes imagine with envy
The lives they wish they had had:
I imagine your life with love now.
(It was I, not you, went mad.)

I wish you a happy autumn
Of a crisp New England sort,
A crunching glitter of sheaves and leaves,
And luck and sport, old sport!

Many Happy Returns

(For each of his children and their mother)

PAUL POTTS

The full value of any poet's work depends on the man inside the poet and not ultimately on the poet within the man. It is meaning and feeling, hurt, happiness and sorrow that will count longer in the end, than rhyme and rhythm and metre. If it was not for what was inside the technique and the sprung rhythm, Hopkins' fame would have not been more than the sensation of a literary season. When the leaves started to fall the absence of the branches would have been noticed. George Barker got off to a good start. His beginning was a triumph. His very earliest poems were praised by Yeats and dismissed by Mr Geoffrey Grigson. His world is a large generous going concern, full of big sixpences within an expanding emotional economy. It is populated with people he has loved and crowded with those who love him. It is irrigated by friends, by his own kind and consanguinity. It is a world revolving around his own hunger, its fixed star his need to love, yet its boundaries are spread abroad between 'the wall of China and my heart'. His world is a long row of confessional boxes where the forgiving priests are his own poems. Rarely is he refused absolution. Each new sin finds another priest. It is a world where, for all his hurry, he is very much alone. Standing sandwiched between oppressor and oppressed. It is a wide world with boundaries in many dimensions. Its first sea was the rain falling on an evicted farmers' face along a country road in County Louth. The vision of England and the news from Spain mix with the scent of Japan and the noise of America. The seasons don't conform to any calendar. The constitution of his republic is the language of the church, yet it is a world always in full rebellion. The man is a poet and he has made his poems out of his life. His muse knows how to forgive. His sins are his sonnets, his litany, his elegies.

George Barker is, together with David Gascoyne and Dylan Thomas, one of the three major poets of my generation. They have actually very little in common beyond the following facts. That they are all very good. That they are poets on a larger scale than their more publicized immediate predecessors were or show any signs of ever becoming. Auden of course is an exception to this. And that their first work was published by the Parton Press. This will cause that small publishing house to be of interest to future literary generations to whom Poetry London and New Writing will convey absolutely nothing. David Gascoyne's most important work may lie in the direction of Kierkegaard and Léon Bloy rather than in that of a lyrical poet, yet there is no body of work in modern English literature by any poet of their decade to compare with that of these three.

Literature is not a competition. Yet poets will invariably be compared with their contemporaries and with their predecessors. Barker's verse is not so perfect as Dylan Thomas's, nor is his vision so intense. Yet his range is wider; his feeling not deeper but more general. For this reason his achievement may not be so obvious, it may not be so completely attained. But if the daisies and the buttercups are plentiful and perfect, a rose is not the less a rose for having a thorn where the petals should be. What really makes a man a real poet except the size of his soul, it is very difficult to say. But it is as equally difficult to fail to realize it, when a writer turns out to be one. George

Barker is, just as surely as Patric Dickinson and Maurice Lind-
say are not. Criticism is really poetry once removed; whereas
poetry is the joy and the understanding of life, so criticism is
the joy and understanding of that poetry.

George Barker is much more difficult to cope with than
either of the other two important poets—Dylan Thomas and
David Gascoyne—of his own literary generation, whose work
was to fill the decade and which was to start out on its journey
with the label of the Parton Press. Dylan Thomas is the easiest
to assess. English poetry, from the beginning until yesterday,
is all one whole, whether it was written by a Dublin clergyman,
Dean Swift or by a New England farmer, Robert Frost; by an
American Negro, Langston Hughes or by a white South
African, Roy Campbell; by a peer of the realm, Byron, or by
an insane pauper, John Clare. In English poetry the adjective
qualifies a language not a place. No one can fully grasp the
immenseness of English poetry without being conscious of
Whitman, of Burns and of Yeats. Dylan Thomas's poems are
the very zenith of that kind of verse in which George Herbert
and Henry Vaughan, Thomas Traherne and John Clare ex-
celled. It is something for our generation to have done so much
so soon. Gascoyne has been more ignored than the two others,
as men of this kind always are, as Kierkegaard and Léon Bloy
were, as Ignazio Silone is. Yet it is easy to see where his fame
lies, what the destination of his muse is to be. George Barker,
however, offers the most difficulty to anyone of this generation
looking at the work of their contemporaries. I am going to
digress for a moment, and I believe that the three men I am
talking about will join me in this digression.

For one of the features of our generation has been the presence in our midst of a large number of European exiles, not all
victims of the Right. And among these were those who were
writers. One of them, Alfred Marnau, who has lived and
worked here for several decades, is a writer whose work forms
a part of the best of the period. 'A Winter's Journey' which

13

forms part of *An Exile's Autobiography* is undoubtedly of a texture made familiar to the readers of the great prose of William Butler Yeats. Alfred Marnau is a very real artist indeed, and his presence in this country added great dignity to the generation to which he belongs.

Unlike any other poet of his generation whose work is at all mentionable in the same sentence as his, George Barker's prose is not of any great stature. It is only fair however not only to Barker, but to any readers this may have, to point out that Edwin Muir's opinion of his prose is quite the opposite. But for one of his readers at least he must stand by his verse alone. The quantity of this is considerable. He wrote what is perhaps the worst book ever to have been written by a real artist, in which it is stated throughout that sex is filthy and she whom you do it with dirty. The name of the book, *The Dead Seagull*. One can never forgive Barker for writing that sort of nonsense, but one can forgive oneself for not being able to forgive him.

His influence in poets younger than himself has been of more use to them and more beneficial than Dylan Thomas's influence on other younger poets. This is probably because he is more in the main stream of English poetry. Whenever one reads Barker, it is almost impossible to avoid the suggestion in one's mind of the cow who kicked over the bucket of milk it had just given. The most natural poem is sometimes spoilt by a stupid pun, like the one in the last line of his huge poem to his mother. Barker is a Byron who hasn't got a Greece. He is a knight errant without a sword, or to be fairer, the sword is there all right but his hand is paralysed by the trouble in his heart. By this it must not be understood that he is unaware of what has taken place during the years which have contained the first half of his writing life. For the most part these happenings find no place in the work of Dylan Thomas. Gascoyne is too much of a mystic to concern himself with the results, his interest is with the causes.

Barker, who has a considerable talent for humanity, has

been left somewhat in the air, not ignoring them, but not being able either to cope with them or to assimilate them into his work. He was too much of an artist to offer us easy slogans. Because his feelings were deeper, because simply he was more of a poet, he didn't jump on to political platforms during the thirties like those poets of the literary generation that immediately preceded his. After all, it took more courage for a poet of Eliot's standing to publish a book about cats than it did for an intellectual to be anti-fascist in a non-fascist country, where the whole public opinion of the circles in which he moved was anti-fascist.

The only artists who organically belong on left-wing political platforms are those like Maxim Gorky, Ignazio Silone, Hugh MacDiarmid and Sean O'Casey, whose work is made from the material out of which socialism itself is carved. It has been said that Barker's *Elegy on Spain*, dedicated to the photograph of a child killed in an air-raid on Barcelona, could just as easily have been written about a child killed by the other side. To which it is correct to answer that any real poem so dedicated would be able to pass through the enemy lines. After all, it wasn't only the Republicans who enjoyed Lorca, let alone one particular brand of Republican. Barker too seems to refute the adage that to be sexually successful is also to be spiritually poverty stricken. One prefers to think of him as one of the many exceptions to a proven rule.

The great thing about the work of a true poet is the atmosphere which it creates in the mind of the reader. This is as difficult to define as it is impossible to miss. It has a great deal to do with technique and style, but only in so far as they are an integral part of the feeling and thinking that go to make up the poet's work. They are of no use or value if they are merely superimposed on top of it. A good bad poet is more of an artist than a bad good poet.

Poetry is a mutual thing, it needs an audience worthy of it. Barker is not everyone's cup of tea, but it is real tea all right,

15

brewed with a mixture of waters, the one from a young clear stream running down the side of an Irish hill, the other the tears of the hunted, and it has been stirred by the poet's own vagrant integrity that never for a moment seems to have been tempted by the prizes of mediocrity. The size of his failures is the measure of his work. Only a real poet could make such huge mistakes. He does not belong to the fixed rows of suburban security so fashionable in some literary circles. As Eliot has recently said of Pound, Barker perpetually gives the impression that he has just packed his bag and is about to move off to some other place. He is a vagrant. The only place where he has a fixed abode is in the poetry of this language. All the requirements of real poetry set forth in the great critical tenets of Coleridge, Walter Savage Landor, John Middleton Murry and Ezra Pound are to be found, without much searching in his verse. Barker may not have built a small, tidy bungalow, but he has already laid the foundations of a huge edifice. His is the carelessness of greatness. He has the sure confidence of a true artist meaning that he is confident about the right things. He is steeped in his craft. He has worked as only a man of enormous vision is capable of working. He may have stopped dead, but he has never wandered off into the alleyways of easy acclaim or polite flattery. He is a victim as any proper writer must always be. Yet he can never escape giving the impression of being in control of his own misfortune. In this he is unlike most of his contemporaries who are as much of an artist as he is.

The literary historian, if not the critic of poetry, will be interested to note that the principal poets of the generation immediately preceding Barker's were all upper middle class, public school and Cambridge or Oxford men. Whereas Thomas, Gascoyne and Barker all finished their schooling somewhere inside the curriculum of various suburban secondary schools. It is also of great interest to note the deep courtesy, real chivalry and true dignity, expressed by them, both in their behaviour and in their writings. When Thomas or Gascoyne writes a love poem, that poem is of its very nature the kind of poem that any man could read to any woman. Compare this, for instance, to the work of some of their contemporaries who were educated at major public schools and senior universities, who in their poems addressed to women and frequently dedicated to them by name, give their readers a geographical survey of that lady's physical charms, whose verse is in fact a publicized Cook's tour of their girl friends' bodies. Poets carry fire in their hands, these people only pack contraceptives into their clichés.

This far has a class fallen. The work of these three poets is proof beyond all question of politics, that the courtesy and good taste of the nation now only exists for the most part in other places than among our governing and privileged and educated classes. No important poet under forty has been to a senior university, no real poet of my generation is what a film script-writer would call a gentleman. Auden, MacNeice and Spender although only a decade or less older than Barker are in a different literary generation altogether, therefore this obviously does not apply to them.

Barker is almost as completely unpolitical as it is possible for a contemporary to be. Yet, like Byron, he goes far beyond the conventional poetic subjects for his material. He is neither as mystical as David Gascoyne nor as religious as Dylan Thomas. The things that worry a politically-concerned person often trouble him. Yet the trouble does not lead to revolt, much less to a desire for power. He wants to understand, sometimes to escape, never to win. He identifies himself with such varied forerunners of St John the Divine and François Villon. He is capable of spoiling a good poem by a noisy line, but never of trying to make one out of any emotion that is not an integral part of his own deep feeling. If Gascoyne gives his readers the impression of a great chef trying to make a feast out of a badly stocked larder, Barker leaves them with the feeling of an

17

ordinary man who is very hungry trying to cook a meal in the kitchen of a king.

George Barker is among the outstanding poets of his generation. That company consists of Thomas and Gascoyne and a far bigger poet than all three of them, Patrick Kavanagh. Barker may have achieved least, but he has certainly suggested a lot; for a man of his age this is part of his achievement. To travel with him is not to arrive, but it is to be very excited about the destination. He may leave one unsatisfied but he has created a hunger that no one else has even suggested.

The world of George Barker is a place for sinners. It is not a street of barricades, nor is it a house where one prays. Yet the nature of the poetry in him is the plentifulness of forgiveness. He is original without being unique. He is very much of this world, in so far as it is a vale of tears, without being seduced by worldliness. His technique is in advance of his maturity. He is married to poetry, he is not just having an affair with words. But he is still waiting for the cock to crow whereas, according to the calendar of his achievements, he should be getting ready for the gift of tongues. If the work of the first half of his writing life can serve as a measuring instrument for the second, he will have proved that Yeats was a good judge of those who were about to begin as he himself was coming to his own great amen. Yet as nearly all creative artists have about fifteen years or so during which they are capable of reaching to the allotted heights of their own intense creation, this may not be his half-way house, it may well be only the front door. Whatever verse, however, his muse may have in reserve for him, and he for the steadily increasing number of his readers, that poetry which he has already written, punctuating as it does his unplanned and wandering journey, proves beyond mere praise that he has embarrassed this language and these years with 'The tremendous gentleness of a poet's kiss'.

The most beautiful story in the whole Barker legend is how, when as a very young man, on arriving home for tea one day, his invalid Irish grandmother, tightly gripping her constant companion, a thin ebony stick with a silver handle, pulled her self up on to her mass-going feet and bowed to him as he entered. In her struggle to rise the book she had been reading dropped to the floor. It was Yeats's *Oxford Book of Modern Verse*; and the youngest poet there included was the grandson who had to kneel in order to pick it up for her.

The first thing that comes into one's mind, after having read his poems, a generous number of which have formed part of the furniture of one's life, is not criticism or even gratitude, but that terribly ancient Hebrew word, Amen, which by reason of long usage is now as native as a cockney's smile, and which being translated means 'and let it be so' and indeed this is not only a first impression but also a final verdict. Then indeed let these poems, this consecrated work of a dedicated man, be just as they are, including their unevenness and their puns. For the undeniable reason, that the man who has made them and who took a quarter of a century to do so (they are going to last a lot longer than that) is a poet to his finger-tips, and he has very long fingers indeed.

These poems are just as English, in the sense that they belong to the community, as were those little white boats, manned by amateur sailors, which rescued an army of professional soldiers, and by so doing probably saved Europe, including Germany, that week between the beaches of Dunkirk and the coasts of Kent. And just as English too as was that unknown private soldier, who, when priests forbade her a crucifix, handed St Joan a home-made cross the day that she was burned. So these poems of his will find their way into what must, in any final assessment, be deemed one of the greatest of human achievements, the literature of the English language.

Note I wrote this at about the time I was ceasing to be a young man, and the editors of this book of deserved tributes, have kindly included it now, just when I am beginning to be an old one. Yet I am leaving it exactly as it was written, although if I had written it last month the emphasis might have been somewhat different. Perhaps, and this of course may easily be more wishful thinking, it could have been more beautifully made. Some so-called critics, who say that George Barker's work does not improve and develop as he grows up, forget—and putting it down to forgetfulness is a charitable way of saying it—that it does not deteriorate either. How many poets are there, in any language, who can make a poem when they are fifty-nine as good as the one they made when they were twenty or even younger?

'To be a poet at twenty is to be twenty; to be a poet at forty is to be a poet.' Paul Potts.

Acrostic Sonnet

for George Barker's Sixtieth Birthday

JOHN FULLER

Gladly as Narcissus leaning towards the lake
Early in April to see the single swan
Out of the rushes beat his wings awake,
Restless as sorrow that guilt moves upon
Giving as to water its buoyancy and ache,
Early you found that looked-for image gone.

But the unknown x entered all your visions
As ruined Europe or the absconded god,
Remaining a corpse about which all decisions
Knelt in useless tears. And with his rod
Eros contrived his eloquent elisions,
Rendering life less horrible and odd.

Long may your pen keep moving for us, your art's
X its equation, the interdependence of parts.

Climbing on Snowdon

for George Barker

THOMAS BLACKBURN

The mountain is higher, the rocks are steeper
As I grow older and penetrate deeper
Into the strata where as once I left water
I must leave this air here and much that I care for.
But leave more myself and somewhat serener
From my traffic in this arduous arena,
As to death I come nearer and knock, a wayfarer
Through what is unknown but may grow clearer
In the strata beyond both air and water
When I bow to meet her, Demeter's daughter.

The Sacred Hearth

to George Barker

DAVID GASCOYNE

You must have been still sleeping, your wife there
Asleep beside you. All the old oak breathed: while slow,
How slow the intimate Spring night swelled through those
　depths
Of soundlessness and dew-chill shadow on towards the day.
Yet I, alone awake close by, was summoned suddenly
By distant voice more indistinct though more distinctly clear
While all inaudible, than any dream's, calling on me to rise
And stumble barefoot down the stairs to seek the air
Outdoors, so sweet and somnolent, not cold, and at that hour
Suspending in its glass undrifting milk-strata of mist,
Stilled by the placid beaming of the adolescent moon.
There, blackly outlined in their moss-green light, they stood,
The trees of the small crabbed and weed-grown orchard,
Perfect as part of one of Calvert's idylls. It was then,
Wondering what calm magnet had thus drawn me from my
　bed,
I wandered out across the briar-bound garden, spellbound.
　Most
Mysterious and unrecapturable moment, when I stood
There staring back at the dark white nocturnal house,
And saw gleam through the lattices a light more pure than gold
Made sanguine with crushed roses, from the firelights that all
　night
Stayed flickering about the sacred hearth. As long as dawn
Hung fire behind the branch-hid sky, the strong
Magic of rustic slumber held unbroken; yet a song
Sprang wordless from inertia in my heart, to see how near

A neighbour strangeness ever stands to home. George, in the
    wood
Of wandering among wood-hiding trees, where poets' art
Is how to whistle in the dark, where pockets all have holes,
All roofs for refugees have rents, we ought to know
That there can be for us no place quite alien and unknown,
No situation wholly hostile, if somewhere there burn
The faithful fire of vision still awaiting our return.

Martin Green—   June 7, 71

George Barker saw William Blake on a tree shining
in Thames' waters before World War II and heard the tree
of poetry babbling in myriad worldly newspaper tongues
prophesying transcendence over the mechanic 'iron woods'
Kali Yugaeoque Apocalypse. Thus gifted with prophecy,
Barker's inspiration was transmitted across the Atlantic and
entered into American poetry along with the Aeonic vowel
mouthings of fellow sensitives Gasgoyne & liquid
sea-tongued Dylan. So American poetry owes him debt
for transmission of living poetic spirit through years of
hot and cold war—Arizonic mentality.
                    Coming to these shores in late Fifties of the
Century, he kissed Peter Orlovsky and bit his tongue by
heaven!

Mr Green—
            This is what's most essential immediately
in mind hommage to George Barker. I am flooded
with papers unfinished work and can't do more
than send these sweet memories.
                                   Yours faithfully,
                                   Allen Ginsberg

ARIZONIC

'handwrit by a friend,' as Allen's
pinkie knuckle is busted)

25

Two Poems

for George Barker

BERNARD SAINT

I

The Singing Sphere

A veiled course keeps this salt and sallow star
Where human longing sears through outstretched hand
  To clarify that light by which all burns.

A course within the poet's heart observes.
Felled by a grief, the levelled eye
Scans man's landscape, learning love
Each creature carries, be it heaven-hurled
Or wrenched from daily tortures with a curse.

We are conspirators
With all that would be holy, all that falls
Moth to the flame
Of vision that will not depart.

Hawk and wren wake to the morning's murder.
Headlines make one flesh of word and pain
As carnage half a world away
Greets us from our whistling in the dark.

Our Muses are of this world, not another.
Fixed within the poet's heartbeat fast,
This singing sphere inspires us in its burning,
Breathes its Beast and Flowered breath of fire,
Encompassing our songs in love's vibrations.

I do not think the singing dies away.
The human heart inhabits its own metaphor.
World's waves that rise in anger, part in peace.

II

A Way of Celebration

All this tall September evening
The dark herbaceous borders of the city
Steep September twilight in a quiet green.
The people pass, unchanged in their element.

Who bear a common heart above the suburbs' waste
Turning, where flights of birds hang in a host
Towards this Autumn's falling husk:
The earth-bound's sound catharsis.

Withdrawn from Summer's heat, their hearts
Must lie alone, unknown but bearing
The clamorous call of a great migration
To a full heart's life or grave.

Poet,
What supreme and hurtling planet can divine
Its fiery soul but by that hub of love
Which you blame-praise?
Hauled in the brake of stars' amoral vapours,
A reverie of moments pass down through the glass
Draining our spirits with it where
The wine evaporates, and we
Stare dumb
Struck on our own reflections.

Who else may move back into light
All men's hearts and his own?
From fathomless night your verse has informed
The filial ear of this indifferent time
A poet's songs may still
Rise up and dance,
Their seven-veiled ironies hung
With supernatural joy;

Renew with vivid and compulsive forms
The people passing by:
The girls whose skirts are bells in Autumn air,
Boys whose Summer has not yet revealed
This urgent celebration in the flames.

Memories of 23A

DAVID WRIGHT

In the late forties and early fifties I was a compulsive dropper-in at 23a Stanhope Gardens, a classical portico'd Victorian terrace house whose front door was framed by one of a row of pairs of white-painted Tuscan columns supporting thumping stone balconies. Quintessential London, of which some specimens may have a fair chance of surviving into the twenty-first century. It stood three minutes' walk from South Kensington tube station, two from the Denmark public-house, five from the Queen's Elm in Brompton Road, and seven from Finch's, further west along the same thoroughfare.

The tenant of its first and second floors (and for all I know its third and fourth, since I never penetrated to the upper regions) was Colonel George Barker, late of the Coldstream Guards, presently Butler to Gray's Inn. It was not the colonel on whom I used to call but the poet, who was not only his son and namesake but physically a perfect impress of the father. The old man would then have been in his late sixties; dark, aquiline, a face reminiscent of Picasso's, baldness augmenting a magnificent forehead; a spare figure, in height between five feet ten and six feet eleven. He was one of those people who, when their wrath is up, do not take thought but add cubits to the stature. Though he never spoke to me except with kindness, and once even advanced a pound note against the security of a very post-dated cheque, I have seen the person of the old

29

man tower with the towering of his dudgeon, literally fill the kitchen-scullery where the family did most of their living, till his head appeared to bump the ceiling. If the bad mood were on him you could feel it two rooms away: an emanation capable on occasion of stretching beyond the house itself, as far as the saloon of the Queen's Elm and the furthest public-bars of Soho. Thoroughly and conventionally the Englishman, he came from a long line of Lincolnshire farmers, had volunteered for the Boer War, fought at Magersfontein and later on the Western Front. He never visited a pub. I have heard that his apocalyptic rages were characteristic of his father, who at midnight when the drink was on him would go into his yard and wrestle with the cattle. It may be for this reason he seldom drank or smoked, and then only fine port and handrolled cigars, samples presented by shippers who supplied the cellars of Gray's Inn.

Many were the Sunday evenings when his sons and I, too broke to raise the price of a half of bitter and a packet of Weights, would gloomily have to substitute his vintage port and Havanas in the scullery for an evening in the public bar of the Denmark.

This kitchen-scullery was the first room you entered after climbing a narrow staircase leading from the ground-floor hall. It was a tall room, not large, one wall of which was almost wholly accounted for by a big sash window overlooking a geometrical limbo of miscellaneous areaways and precincts. A gas stove reposed opposite, leaving the remaining space for a large round kitchen-table where the family had breakfast, lunch, tea, and supper, despite the existence of an official dining-room just round the corner. This was a rather sombre chamber, usually unlit and never used except for great feasts like a wedding or Christmas. A solid mahogany dining table stood in a corner, a chair or two by an unlighted fireplace, while the far wall, opposite the window, was almost entirely occupied by a huge oil canvas, Aztec in theme, inhabited by angular

30

stylized forms and figures picked out in barbaric colour. Dominating and completely out of place, this work seemed to threaten the other furniture. But the dining-room was less a room than a foyer—an interval, tenebrous but grandiose, between the kitchen-scullery and the large, splendidly-proportioned sittingroom whose three tall French windows opened on a narrow stucco balcony facing the street. A chinese room: huge dragon-enfolded jars and vases, chinoiserie lampshades, screens, and peacock feathers. Comfortable plump-cushioned sagging armchairs and an engulfing sofa besieging a marble-browed coal-burning fireplace defended by brass fire-irons. Here the old man, when the lightning wrapped him, would sit solitary. But in my mind it is to Mrs Barker, Big Momma, that the room belonged, for in it I first met her, huge as Asia, clustered with grandchildren and daughters, and it was there I last saw her, upright in a chair facing the french windows, and beside her a plate of elevenses, teacakes cased in pink fancy icing, untouched on the table.

As Irish as the old man was English, she came from Drogheda, of which port her father, a Taaffe, had been pilot; his pilot's certificate hung framed in her kitchen.

In this kitchen she reigned throughout the day—a room I cannot remember ever seeing empty, and which must in fact have been much larger than memory supposes, for besides Big Momma there were never less than two of her children, or of her children's children, her children's friends and her children's children's friends . . . There she would be with her back to the dresser and the teapot with a grubby cosy to it on the table:

—Will you have a cup o' tay?

solid as mother earth, gregarious, generous, but not soft, well able to shut the door on a face she didn't like. But if there were a cloud over the day or in your face, and she had the stuff, in handing your teacup she would reach under the table, pull out a bottle of gin and pour in a good dollop. Though there was

31

always plenty of eating and drinking going on I can't remember much cooking itself being done in the kitchen, except on those days when she would turn to and produce, with no apparent interruption of the kitchen's normal role of Clapham Junction for the household and its callers, one of her enormous brown-flaked steak and kidney pies. There was little she knew about art and poetry, and little she didn't about artists and poets; after all, she had mothered both. She had three daughters, all married with children, and two sons: the elder a poet, the younger a painter. The great Mexican canvas in the dining-room was Kit's. It was to see this picture that I had first called at 23a one winter evening in 1947, some time after I had first met George Barker and Elizabeth Smart in a Younger's pub off Rathbone Place. Tambimuttu, that professional catalytic agent, had found me in the nearby Wheatsheaf and asked if I would like to meet George Barker. Would I not? He for me and many was a magnetic legend, like Byron; a mysterious absentee in America, from whence he had returned, bleeding from wounds and wives . . .

Much has been written about the Dylan Thomas legend. But Dylan, in the Soho circles where he operated, was more in the nature of a happening. George Barker, on the other hand, cast his shadow before him. In the fifties, when he lived near Haslemere in a remote cottage,* he would sporadically, without warning or system, come up to London for a night or two. Soho, by then, had drifted far to the south of Rathbone Place and was already lapping against the spiritual boundary of Shaftesbury Avenue. But on those nights when George was

---

* Remote from roads and houses that is. A couple of journalists from the *News Chronicle*, trying to interview him after Lord Balfour of Inchrye had been lambasting the BBC in the House of Lords for encouraging pornography by allowing the Third Programme to broadcast *The True Confession of George Barker*, had to abandon their car, sunk to its axletrees in the middle of a bog, when they attempted to reach this cottage.

'up' the pubs in the environs of Old Compton Street would crowd with his friends and disciples, mysteriously assembled by some form of ESP or telepathic tocsin. It was a phenomenon I often experienced. About six or seven on any given evening one 'knew', felt in one's bones as it were, that he would be around that night. Sure enough, by nine o'clock in the Pillars of Hercules, the French, or the public bar of the Duke of Wellington, whichever was the establishment in favour at the period, one would find George Barker, tartan-shirted, slightly hunched, standing at the mahogany counter in the middle of a mob of poets and painters, similarly summoned, who would have come, as I did, to listen and participate in some of the best talk in London, comic and profound, passionate and humorous. I for one owed a large part of my education, not only in poetry, to these gatherings.

But all this was in the future. That first meeting with George Barker in the extra-territorial pub (reached from the Wheatsheaf by a narrow winding brick alley, sinisterly lit with ancient gas lamps fixed to the walls on rusting iron brackets) was, like most first meetings, stiff and useless. But it was followed by chance encounters in the plaid-hung Wheatsheaf, where George would occasionally turn up in his cap and blue naval pea-jacket, among such characters as Jimmy Burns Singer, the painter Jankel Adler, Paul Potts, the king of Poland in his crown and gown, J. Maclaren-Ross with malacca cane and millionaire's overcoat, and the old lady at her corner table doing the *Evening News* crossword with a bottle of Guinness. One day the word-magician (for so he was and is) accepted and even kept an engagement to tea in my small flat above a bombed electric appliance shop in Great Ormond Street. Where he talked only of his brother Kit's paintings; and invited me to call at 23a to see them. And so it was that I came round one evening, lonely and dark and November, cold too, and rang, not untrepidantly, that unfamiliar bell; which was answered, not by George, who had by then vanished in the direction of

Ireland, but by one of his sisters whom I had never met, who did not listen to my stumbling phrases of explanation but pulled me in through the passage and stifled blackness of the dining-room foyer into the great Chinese sitting-room, crackling with a blazing fire, full of people, whose centripetal point of warmth and light was that great woman whom I recognized at once from the famous sonnet

> Irresistible as Rabelais but most tender for
> The lame dogs and hurt birds that surround her
> She is a procession no one can follow after
> But be like a little dog following a brass band.

Impossible to describe Big Momma without paraphrasing and spoiling her son's poem; it is only possible to attest its— accuracy I was going to write, but veracity is the proper word. There is a line in it:

> Gin and chicken helpless in her Irish hand

which I was later to see embodied in that sitting-room at one of the parties, I think for Kit's wedding, parties seldom but explosively permitted (Mr Barker senior being acquiescent but absent) at which were present riff-raff like myself from the Rathbone Place pubs—the two Roberts, Colquhoun and Mac-Bryde, David Archer, Johnny Minton, the three Bernards, Oliver, Bruce, and Jeff, Michael Hamburger, wandering Americans—and, of course, a vast miscellanea of Barkers and their ramifications, aunts, cousins, nephews, nieces, in-laws. There she sat, just as it says in the poem, a glass of gin in one hand, a chicken sandwich shaking in the other, oscillant, hilarious . . .

If she had a fault it was that of being too magnetic a mountain. Maternal, gregarious, she moved in a surround of her children and their families. Now and then she might make a state visit to the Queen's Elm—in those days a less self-consciously bohemian establishment—when la famille Barker would turn out in force. A whole army in fact: for on one of these occasions I recall being in its far corner, wedged against the counter and the partition dividing the saloon and public bars, and suddenly realizing (I was talking with George at the time and he had turned aside to buy a round) that as far as the eye could reach I could see nobody but Barkers; I counted twenty-seven before the arrival of a glass of beer turned my head and mind back to the conversation.

The household, naturally, was a dichotomy, a dialectic between the absolute decorous Englishness of the father and the absolute Irishness of the mother. For the one (it is perfectly understandable) irresponsible revelry and improvident bohemia were anathemata—where would it all end—while the other lived, as Wordsworth has it, in what alone is ours, the living Now. Christmas was the crunch—the old man's idea of this festivity being traditionally English, a turkey dinner at home confined to the family (goodness knows that was sizable enough); Big Momma's, to invite all and sundry, waifs and strays, the more the merrier; and both, despite the mutual experience of forty years, would assume that the other's notion of The Day jibed with his or hers . . . As often as not all went well, but Christmases there were when it didn't, and the old man stamped out of the house, on one occasion locking, or forgetting to unlock, the cupboard with the drinks in it . . . He had, of course no faith in painting or poetry as a future for his sons; even the fame of his eldest (which came early) counted for nothing. I do not mean it was no matter of pride, but that he could see in it no guarantee of pecuniary security. Against this responsible lack of faith was set his wife's intuitive magnanimity, a trust not sanguine but responsive to those values which are the true ones but have no price tickets on them. Though the old man, on this account, appears the less sympathetic, I did not know then, and I do not know now, which of the two of them, finally, I admired the more.

The Litany of Satan

A translation of Baudelaire for George Barker

JAMES LIDDY

You most sophisticated most beautiful angel
Divinity betrayed

Satan have mercy on my long misery.

Prince in unjust exile
Stronger more lovely in defeat and failure

Satan have mercy on my long misery.

Inspirer of the underground
Binder-up of the agonies that make us human

Satan have mercy on my long misery.

To outcasts by sickness or through the laws
You teach through love taste for Paradise

Satan have mercy on my long misery.

Through your brave lover Death
You bring the pure madness of hope

Satan have mercy on my long misery.

You give to criminals the haughty gaze
That condemns a nation around a scaffold

Satan have mercy on my long misery.

You know in what corners of envious lands
Jealous God hid the precious stones (of happiness)

Satan have mercy on my long misery.

Your bright eye discovered the armoury
Where the vaulted tribe of metals sleep

Satan have mercy on my long misery.

Your vast hand screens the precipice from
The sleepwalker at the edge of high buildings

Satan have mercy on my long misery.

By magic you make supple the old bones
Of the bewildered drunk fallen under horses

Satan have mercy on my long misery.

You console mankind who is always nervous
By mixing saltpetre and sulphur

Satan have mercy on my long misery.

You make your mark accomplice
On the forehead of the vile employer of labour

Satan have mercy on my long misery.

You lure young girls to Bohemia
The cult of the wound filthy clothes

Satan have mercy on my long misery.

Spear of the exile lamp of inventors
Confessor of traitors and the hanged

Satan have mercy on my long misery.

Adopted father of those whom in his black rage
God the Father chased from earthly paradise

Satan have mercy on my long misery.

Prayer

Glory and honour to you in clouds of Heaven
When you glittered there and in the circles
Of Hell where a failure you dream in silence.
Grant one day my soul will rest beside yours
Under the Tree of Knowledge when like a Temple
Its branches will greenly spread.   Amen.

To George Barker on his Sixtieth Birthday

PAUL DURCAN

In Spring my father goes to the wars
And in Summer he dies
But October brings him home
It is only Winter that will not change
For we never can find the same gold twicc

To George Barker on his Sixtieth Birthday

JOHN HEATH-STUBBS

Now that brash and brazen careerists usurp
The belly or the saddle of the winged or wooden horse,
Nothing, but nothing at all, would give me to speak
But this imperative to celebrate, and your bark entering
The circumpolar seas.

                 Time was, when I thought I had that gift
(And maybe I had) you were the good barker
Snapping at my heels, Anubis
Dogging my footsteps through the tunnels of the dead.
Now that is over, and I walk in the common daylight
(And I am glad that I do) I mark you striding
Under a sun, if cadent to the West,
Yet fervent still to melt
The petrifactions of the Gorgon and
The bombinant Chimæra (and am glad that I do).

Memories of George Barker

from 'A Rebel in the 30s'

MAURICE CARPENTER

A persistent memory remains of George Barker, a young poet with a beautiful profile and flashing eyes, taking out a book one night in the Wheatsheaf, in Rathbone Place, as he sat at the long oaken table.

'So you want to hear some poetry,' he said with a flourish. He began reading:

> Oh there is blessing in the gentle breeze
> That blows from the green fields and from the clouds
> And from the sky; it beats against my cheek,
> And seems half conscious of the joy it gives.
> O welcome messenger! Oh welcome friend!
> A captive greets thee, coming from a house
> Of bondage, from your City's walls set free
> A prison where he long hath been immured. . . .

The room was hushed. The drinkers filled the seats round the long table. Even Julian MacLaren-Ross, in his teddy-bear coat at the head of the bar, ceased to speak. The Roberts, Colquhoun and MacBryde, were acknowledging the existence of English poetry.

I do not think George can have given us the whole of 'The Prelude', but while he was reading heads leaned on elbows,

41

flopped down on the table. The walls vanished. The city, so fair from Westminster Bridge in early morning a hundred and fifty years before, so foul since, had gone. The soft rain and air of Cumberland invaded that chamber. We were snatched away with him, transported, before we returned to the dreary drinking round. Wheatsheaf, Marquis, Black Horse, and across the road to the Highlander, that stayed open until eleven. Then one of the drinking clubs and the Covent Garden Market pubs in the morning.

But George, with his young brother, had packed his traps, to set forth in his old rattling car to his (George's) cottage in Dorset. And I went with them.

He would buy these old bangers, Austin sevens or bull-nosed Morris eights, for above a fiver. George and Kit had always been fascinated by motor cars, and these old crocks were their delight.

It was the early spring of 1934, in a Morris Cowley piled high with tables, beds, crockery, stoves, all the young Barker's worldly goods, George, his wife Jessica, Kit and I, for their new cottage in Plush Bottom, on a hill above Piddletrenthide.

The car had no horn or warning signal, but I had just acquired a trumpet. I could not drive, and never, in spite of this, learned to drive, and my contribution to the journey was long, loud shrill blasts that made pedestrians jump out of the way.

We rattled through Dorset lanes listening for big ends about to go. The orchards were in flower, acre upon acre of blossom. We vowed to come back scrumping in the autumn.

We did so, to find those orchards a carpet of apples. What a waste! we said, stowing the apples under the floor boards of the car. We did not know they were cider apples, left to lie there until they were shovelled into the presses. Until we bit into one, and felt the mouth retreat in a panic of dried up sour disgust.

We bought bread cheese and onion from the little shop in

Piddletrenthide. These villages are strung along the Piddle (or Puddle) valley, Alfs Piddle, Bryans Piddle, Piddlehinton and Piddletrenthide, Puddletown and Tolpuddle, renowned for the famous martyrs.

I had to get out and swing the starting handle in Piddle-trenthide. This service I, non-driver, was constrained to do. George put the car in gear, let out the clutch and we started up the hill to Plush. It was a steep winding hill, about one in six.

At the steepest bit there was an ominous clanking noise and the engine stalled. Nothing Kit or George could do induced it to go on. We let the car run back to a bend, turned round, and free-wheeled down to Abbott's garage in Piddletrenthide. Arthur Abbott pushed his cap back, took a cursory glance and said (as he had said several times before, and would say many times again):

'Ah well! 'Er be a dead 'un er be!'

And we toiled on foot up the hill to the cottage. The big end or half-shaft was gone, and was hardly worth repairing. On the only occasion when we arrived intact, Arthur, on the next occasion, let the petrol nozzle fall on the magneto, knocking out the timing so that he could make the classic reply:

'Ah well! 'Er be a dead 'un er be.'

The proper address of the cottage was not Plush Bottom, but The Butts, Plush, Folly, Mappowder, Piddletrenthide, Dorset. This trio of villages was the country of the gentle philosopher novelist Theodore F. Powys (author of *Mr. Weston's Good Wine*). It was near Cerne Abbas, protected by the phallic figure of the Cerne giant, to whom the local maidens, to the distress of the vicar, used to pray.

In the spring of 1934 the Butts smelled sooty and damp, but we soon had a bright fire blazing in the big old fashioned range. We sat round the blaze, munching, drinking, and talking brilliantly. We had a flagon of cider from the Plush Arms that in those days never had more than one customer, though later, during war time, it became a rendezvous of the rich for its incredible store of liquor during those years of shortage.

We exulted in our first discovery of William Blake; 'The Mental Traveller', that incredible cycle of human birth and death, revealed for the first time in all its magnificence and terror.

And if the babe is born a boy
It's given to a woman old
Who nails him down upon a rock
Catching his shrieks in cups of gold . . .

George Barker in 1934 was an imperious young man with a roman nose, a sensual rather feminine mouth and that rare curio the bar of Michael Angelo he mentions in his first, auto-biographical novel, *Alanna Autumnal*. We immediately took to one another, he assuming the role of bully, older brother, brilliant expositor, intimate cajoler, and I, the listener, admirer, sufferer and mirror, though I was in fact two years older than he was.

He introduced me to his mother and father, the Gargamelian Irishwoman and the straight ex-guardsman, ex-policeman whose tall stories outdid Munchausen. And his vociferous, beautiful, happy go lucky sisters who enlivened all those days.

Yet George's preoccupations were suicide and death. He was evolving from his catholic childhood and the works of Cardinal Newman his own philosophy of the uselessness and fundamental repulsiveness of all human activity. I was worried about him. His predicament clouded all my days. Even David Archer at the Parton Street bookshop noticed something was wrong. He asked me about it.

'I'm sure George is going to kill himself,' I said. David emitted a most un-Archerlike guffaw.

I was furious. I picked up a full bottle of ink and hurled it across the shop at him. George's despair and disgust with life were to carry him through a dozen or so books of verse and three novels.

It was a bright spring day the year before that George was having coffee with David Archer in Meg's, across the road from the bookshop. At a corner by himself, withdrawn into silence sat a man with a magnificent head. He had once been known as Colonel Lawrence.

George picked up the menu and began to scribble the lines:

> O to us speak
> Bleak snow
> With your mellifluous smooth voice.

That was the beginning of *Thirty Preliminary Poems* published by the Parton Press, the forerunner of an immortal succession of books.

Apology for the Revival of Christian Architecture in England

GEOFFREY HILL

Sanctified by such passages
Let us exchange our messages . . .

GEORGE BARKER

I

Ambrose defected; you stayed and were sure,
fervent in reason, watchful of his name:
his signet-seal's unostentatious gem
gleams against walnut on the escritoire,

focus of reckoning and judicious prayer.
This is the durable covenant, a room
quietly furnished with stuff of martyrdom,
lit by the flowers and moths from your own shire,

by silvery vistas frothed with convolvulus—
radiance of dreams hardly to be denied.
The chirruping pipistrelle, so strange and close,

plucks its curt flight through the moist eventide;
the children thread among old avenues
of snowberries, clear-calling as they fade.

II

Stroke the small silk with your whispering hands,
godmother; nod and nod from the half-gloom;
broochlight intermittent among the fronds,
the owl immortal in its crystal dome.

46

Along the mantelpiece veined lustres trill,
the clock discounts us with a telling chime.
Familiar dynasties, clerks-of-appeal,
burnish upon the threshold of the dream:

churchwardens in wing-collars, bearing scrolls
of copyhold well-tinctured and well-tied.
Your photo-albums loved by the boy-king

preserve in sepia waterglass the souls
of distant cousins, virgin till they died,
and the lost delicate suitors who could sing.

III

High voices in domestic chapels; praise;
praise-worthy feuds; far-dreamed-of spires that sprung
crisp-leaved as though from dropping-wells. The young
ferns root among our vitrified tears.

What an elopement that was: the hired chaise
tore through the fir-grove, scattered kinsmen flung
buckshot and bridles, and the tocsin swung
from the tarred bellcote dappled with dove-smears.

Wires tarnish in gilt corridors, in each room
stiff with the bric-a-brac of loss and gain.
Love fled, truly outwitted, through a swirl

of long-laid dust. Today you sip and smile
though still not quite yourself. Guarding its pane
the spider looms against another storm.

© 1973 by Geoffrey Hill

Two Imitations

MARTIN GREEN

I
On Reading George Barker's 'On a
Distant Prospect of Downing College'

My dear, Geor
geous darling Bar
ker no ass sure
to lash your par
tners incrimin
ological
ity whose hides
you flay o so
mercilessly

But surely gran
dad of my ville
wise maker of
majestic rill
you've used a sledge
to hammer nuts
when a hedge switch
could have made cuts
much deeper still?

II
On Seeing George Barker in a Mercedes Benz

I saw four horsemen riding by
Of the apocalypse
Their backs were wet, their lips were dry
The sun was in eclipse.

I stood in the burning sand
Alone as lone could be:
'What's the news, is someone dead
Is there news to set men free?'

The fourth of the four horsemen
As he went riding by
He took a horse-whip from his side
And lashed me in the eye.

Rome's Rake

KARL MILLER

I wrote about George Barker in the *New Statesman* seven
years ago, when *The Dead Seagull* was reissued and the two
parts of *The True Confession* were put together in the one book.
I find that these are the words I still want to use about him.
This, more or less, is what I wrote . . .

George Barker's 'malady is an ingrowing soul; his virtue,
that he has diagnosed it. His prescription is—Excess: he will
rage himself out.' Thus, in 1934, *Scrutiny*: strangely approving,
some might suppose (the reviewer was Hugh Gordon Porteus).
Some might also suppose that the interest of this old rager is
now defunct. I don't agree, though no doubt part of the
interest is nostalgic. Here are pages, however, which only a
good writer could hope to cause.

> What does one fear when one awakes in the morning? Is it
> the day, with its major temptations and minor renuncia-
> tions, its afternoon misdemeanours, the sins that come up
> sighing out of the twilight, the suicide that smiles down at
> one from the midday sun, the death of a favourite dog at a
> quarter past three, the resolution that will get itself born
> at an unpropitious conjunction of monsters, stars and
> houses?

Such prose, with its Latin polysyllables, its personifications
('Love', 'Existence'), its swizzling metaphors ('Turn in my

50

wounds like a knife in a grave'), is so rankly of its time that for many it must rank as an old friend or flame. This is the prose of *The Dead Seagull*, more of an oration than a novel, and a work which, like Elizabeth Smart's *By Grand Central Station I Sat Down and Wept*, memorialises a world of 20 years ago. Both are relics of the vanished Apocalyptic movement, both are manuals of Excess, or Extravagance, and both are currently unfashionable.

Mr Barker's writing moves between extremes of the euphuistic, or Excessive, and the occasional: that's to say, a vein of semi-satirical, conversational poetry, a poetry of social observation and social observance, capable of public gestures of a sort and quite likely to carry a dedication to a particular person. The well-known poem to his mother is occasional. He has never given his second talent sufficient rein—he who has given rein to so much—and while *The True Confession* must be regarded as occasional too, it's not a good example. Certainly its *success* is highly occasional. The catastrophic incoherence of the verse is a matter of intention—Mr Barker is a student of catastrophe, a veteran. Too often, though, the doggerel, far from serving as an idiom fit for a magnificent mongrel, is just plain dead doggerel, and there are too few lucid intervals of incantation, though he weeps like an angel at times, as well as like a crocodile. All this is a loss, coming from one who can write, often enough, like both Byrons: he can go no more a-raging, and he can be like Don Juan. In contrast, *The Dead Seagull* is euphuistic. Yet the two books are alike in that they are partly of the same period, and conduct you round the stations of the same catastrophe. They also share one almighty common concern: what to do with God. It would appear that along with his mistrust of the social there was a growing inclination to take shelter in the theological. I don't recall that you can detect this, exactly, in his early work.

My mother warned me about George Barker when I was a boy, explaining that he wrote 'Papist propaganda'. This seemed wrong, at the time. But *Propaganda*? A kind of rhyming Father D'Arcy? Get away with you. Re-reading these books, however, indicates that I must make amends, that my mother was, up to a point, right.

'We had both been born and educated in the Roman Church,' says *The Dead Seagull*'s narrator of himself and his bride: the novel tells how he betrays her with a many-splendoured witch named Marsden and how she dies in childbirth. The casual reader might be pardoned for taking the book to mean that sex is sin and so is birth, which in turn begets more sex. One of Mr Barker's poems contains the lines:

> The love that kisses with a homicide
> In robes of generation resurrects.

The fatal kiss is then resumed. On the pregnant body of the narrator's wife could be observed 'the measurable dimensions of sin', and he himself refers to 'the homicidality of love', suggesting that the sexual act is wholly conditioned by the treasons and aggressions that frequently attend it. Spelt out, or taken literally, or one stage further, these teachings would be bound to put a lot of people off; Barker would seem to rhyme with Dracula. Others may decide that they are a crazy way of celebrating the importance, and drama, of the sexual life. Better this than the 'life-giving, cheery' view whose absence Eliot once applauded in Baudelaire; or than the sensible, tonic view of Aha!-sayers like Wayland Young and Alex Comfort. Much of the present debate about sex might have been designed to do it an injury, or at least to belittle it. George Barker, with his 'nine-tiered tigresses', has never tried to do the latter. As he might himself claim, his writings are its trophies, its bleeding scalps, however much he can fairly be blamed for showing off and making mysteries on the subject.

The Dead Seagull is a way of saying what it is to have been reared in the Church; it is a preposterous, lingering farewell to the Catholic God, a tribute—suitably expressed in Baroque terms, with lapses into Grand Guignol—to its perseverance in the mind of the guilty backslider; it is a sheaf of anxiety dreams about the calamities and assassinations that define all forms of infidelity. The lapses, the touches of farce, are no hazard, but actually take the curse off some of it: it would not do for the poet to emerge looking just like St Paul or even Cardinal Newman—I imagine he'd prefer Dracula to that. Neither St Paul nor Cardinal Newman could ever have written 'Wherever I arrive I find my life in flames.'

That account was written in 1965. The mention of my mother's warning might have induced me to refer to another warning—received from Gypsy George himself, when I was a student: modesty, perhaps, forbade. We were staying with a friend who is now dead, John Farrelly, at Forte dei Marmi in Italy. We were in a bar, around noon. George told the girl I later married that I should be kept in an attic, and fed on buns, and be made to avoid conventional jobs, so that I might concentrate on writing: 'That boy has a tiger in his loins.' Why do I report this accolade? Because it is comical, and typical, and because it shows a generosity in him. I gathered he was sending me up a bit, but he was also giving encouragement to a young man, and in a way that was bound to appeal to him: earlier, he'd given instructions on how to train, and ride, the tiger. That piece of advice has a period interest too: it's a piece of what might be called (after the king as well as the poet) Georgiana. It speaks of a time when sex and writing were reckoned to be dangerous and very important. The high-risk homicides who thought so are disappearing now, that particular *vie de bohème* has more or less gone, and I expect that young people consider such attitudes incomprehensible and outlandish, and, of course, male-chauvinistic. In the Forties there were many who considered George Barker a show-off, and an exploiter of antediluvian fears, but even they seemed to know what he meant. Even those who were keen to deny that Eros was sinful knew what he meant.

At the present time some of those who are sure that the sexual act is without sin have taken to behaving as if it were also without importance. I don't assume that this helps to prove that George was right about these matters. And, for my own part, I don't believe that potency is a crime. But I was taught that it was, and I learnt the lesson better than I knew. George wrote for all tigers who had learnt that lesson, including those who had come to repudiate it.

He gave a piece of advice once to another student, and perhaps that should also be reported. The student was pouring out a bottle of beer for him, none too well. 'Tilt it, boy, tilt it,' said George. 'Tilt everything in life.' Few of the guilty tigers and tilters who read his work in the Forties had any trouble deciphering the message of this agent of the Vatican. Here was a new way of saying that religion could be erotic and sex religious. If, for some of those concerned, the Supreme Pontiff acquired a tigerish tilt which he has never lost, this rogue-Catholic poet and potentate was largely responsible.

Historia Naturalis

for George Barker

PETER LEVI

In the island of old men
rivers are green and the sea is clear water:
their hands are yellow leaf
their legs are scaly
they have the breath and blood-colour of swans.

In the island of young men
grass heaves under enormous trees:
their hands are brambles
they smell of bitter smoke
they hunt like cats along the empty beaches.

In the island of old women
the trees have fruited, jam has been made:
their hands are water-herbs
their legs are poplars
their bodies bowl in the wind like thunder-clouds.

In the island of young women
nothing is quite in flower but shadows:
their hands are a moth, a descent of snow
their knees are the face of a bird
in sleep they are the steady falling of rain.

In the islands of the past
the small hands of the monkeys in the ruins
feed poets who always look astonished.
The poets live uneasily
inscribing stones,
their eyes are thirsty for sand.
Horizons eat away horizons.
There is understanding in the eyes of the monkeys.
Maybe we have no future.

Prolegomenon to George Barker

PATRICK SWIFT

I

Central to the Romantic view, since it relies heavily on the operations of personality, is its notion of the character and function of the poet. In this it tends to exalt the poet as creator (ποιητής), as opposed to his role as workman (τεχνίτης). Its fiercest opposition being to those who would make a science of art or of man.

In terms of emphasis this at once brings it into conflict with elements in the attitude of those of us deeply affected by what can be broadly called the modern movement (I am thinking of Art which places its faith in things more than in ideas, and which tends to reduce the status of subject).

I do not write in the role of historian, but it is helpful, since in the work of Barker the question of the poet's character is important, to recall something of the genesis of the romantic idea of the poet. The more so since in an age and society dominated by the concept (and fact) Job, it has been one of Barker's functions to assert the purity of the true poet.

It was in a Europe haunted by the intellect of Lord Byron, and already uneasy about the impending horrors of Democracy, that this idea of the poet was born. By Europe I mean the conscious European mind (i.e. Stendhal, Delacroix, etc).

The poetic imagination, confronted by the first wave of the universal assault on the supremacy of the Personal, found its defence in the concept of the Dandy.

For this it was directly indebted to Byron, though it had to await Baudelaire for its proper definition and exposition.* The freedom conferred by this attitude of mind was in fact a mechanism whereby the poet could survive the increasing humiliations that necessarily attended his intercourse with a mephitic society. His strength lay in his consciousness of his high vocation.

In this way the importance of inspiration comes to be asserted. It is in the superior, if terrible, quality of his fate and function that he finds the compensations necessary to survival. His is obeying a higher power within, and ultimately this power is itself his subject matter. In fact his own Dementia, as Auden has pointed out.

Such a position, with its apparent arrogance must in the end rely on ethics for its strength. It is probable that all art must do so, but in this case it is vital, since without clear moral authority the romantic poet is ridiculous. If he owes his superiority merely to himself being himself, and if the voices he obeys are in reality all his own voice, then he must think himself God, or the voice of God, in order to justify his claims. He must find an authority to which to relate the profound importance which he claims for the imagination, or appear simply a lunatic.

It is of the essence of the romantic position that it is not absolute or static. It is driven by the necessities of its own nature to evolve an ethos and find a god.

Christianity, and one might say more precisely Augustinian

* It is the idea of heroic reaction against corruption: '. . . beaux, lions ou dandys, tous sont issus d'une même origine; tous participent du même caractère d'opposition et de révolte; tous sont des représentants de ce qu'il y a de meilleur dans l'orgueil humain, de ce besoin, trop rare chez ceux d'aujourd'hui, de combattre et de détruire la trivialité. . . . Le dandysme apparait surtout aux époques transitoires où la démocratie n'est pas encore toute-puissante, où l'aristocratie n'est que partialement chancelante et avilie.'—*Le Peintre de la Vie Moderne*. Baudelaire.

Christianity, offers a tolerable haven to the romantic madman. His reaction may be occasionally blasphemous when he acknowledges it. But it is doubtful if the history of ideas offers any better alternative. I am thinking of the Christian notion of the Logos, and particularly Augustine's exposition of the activity of the logos within the individual breast. I am going to suggest that it will be useful to look at Barker as a Catholic Christian, or as a romantic driven from the wilderness of his initial position towards a position that is Catholic and Christian. I do not, however, suggest that this is the whole story.

Nietzsche has said 'at the heart of every philosophy is the moral and the moral is the man'. It would be my contention that this is even truer of poetry, and that it is particularly so in the case of George Barker.

II

'J'ai cultivé mon hysterie avec jouissance et terreur.' This remark by Baudelaire might well have come from Barker. It relates closely to his view of the character of the poet, which is mantic, Sybilline, Dionysian, in fact mad—in character lunatic, but distinguished from the merely insane by a quality of moral dedication: 'one could, with some truth, call a lunatic a poet without intentions, and a poet a lunatic with intentions.'

In the poet lives, in schizoid unease, on the one hand the natural man (lunatic), and on the other the moral maniac with a vision of innocence, but the poet himself is not simply one or other of these. Nevertheless, it is the moral element that transforms the otherwise merely mad into the responsible.

There is only one kind of development possible for the poet and that is moral, a progress that is not so much onward and upward (as with christian soldiers etc.) as downward and inward. The position of the romantic poet is not romantic but at all times ethical, for like the happily married man of Kierkegaard he is only happily married as long as he is happily

59

married. Should he awake one morning and find himself unhappy in his marriage or no longer married, he has no more right to the title than if like many other men he had never married or had merely unhappily married etc. In fact the poet preserves his existence only by a constant effort of renewal.

This renewal is in the simplest terms a development of taste. I present this phrase in the sense with which Eugene Delacroix endowed it. This refinement as seen in the verse of Barker has had a more or less constant direction.

The play *In the Shade of the Old Apple Tree* places him so close to the orthodox Catholic view of good and evil, that he may as well be called a 'Catholic' poet.

Catholic philosophy is a philosophy of human failure. Its most serious aspect is that of disillusion in the possibilities for happiness in this life. It offers only the hope of salvation after death, and the great difficulty for the poet would seem to be that whereas he can enter fully into the pessimism of the view of life involved, it is not at all easy for him to get a passionate grasp of the idea of good and of ultimate reward.

Barker's view of the Evil one, 'the downward demon pull', suffers a gradual refinement of definition over the twenty-five years covered by the collected poems.

There is not however any clear vision of the nature of beatitude and no notion of redemption, that one could seriously believe in, emerges.*

What becomes clearer and more constantly present, explicitly and in underlying feeling, is the vision of

> That desert of human loves
> Individual loneliness

* This remark may leave out an element in the more recent poems, most evident in *Goodman Jacksin and the Angel*, which is the effort to reconcile the persistence of good and evil paradoxically, so that from apparent evil comes good

> Out of that fouled and rocking nest . . .
> Out, out the innocent image steps

60

In this play there is the inevitability of sin and betrayal, and the dreadful consciousness of this inevitability.

The question of Original Sin is clearly at the heart of Barker's vision. And we are not far away from the world of Charles Baudelaire here. The world of *Les Fleurs de Mal*, and perhaps more of the diaries and the criticism. There is the same view of sin, and this is related to a view of the sexes as divided by their ethical position; man living in relation to an absolute, cursed by a sense of the ideal, woman living entirely in a world of relationships.*

The position of pride and of ego, the 'satanic I am', the recognition that prayer occupies a higher category than the poem, the view of poetry as what Jacques Rivière has called a 'raid on the absolute and its results a revelation,' all are common to Barker and Baudelaire.

There is also Baudelaire's famous concern with correspondences and his view of the character of true intelligence in this respect. For Barker the correspondences constitute the key to poetic profundity, that is, the poem is profound in terms of what it conceals, for the multiplicity of faces behind the mask which it apparently consists of.

The image is for him the discovered fact of the imagination.

> What Michelangelo saw hidden in a piece of dirt . . . what Jehovah forbids made of himself because when the image has been given to a thing or an idea then the thing or idea has been subjugated. The image is made up of words, words are made up of the alphabet, and the alphabet is the twenty-six stations of the cross to the Logos.

> The poem is what happens to the image.

In experiencing 'the multiplicities or correspondences that the image conceals' he discovers that 'the poetry is the

* I have always been astonished that women are allowed to enter churches. What conversation can they have with God?

Mon Cœur Mis à Nu, LXXI

61

correspondent'. Thus the poem is the special agent whose function is to 'arrogate the unknowable'. It is the instrument of the imagination which seeks to honour and acknowledge the absolute. The poem will always conceal more than it discloses. To rule out the numinous would be totally to degrade the role of the poem and of the poet.

I am attempting to get a view of Barker's notion of the function of the poem and of the poet's responsibility in this light. It is necessary because in this lies the positive and 'good' aspect of his vision. It does not lie in a logically held conception of spiritual salvation. Pierre Jean Jouve has said 'Dans le mot, le poète se sauve, et point autrement'. But the poet is not an impartial observer, nor the counsellor of conscience, he is a participant, i.e. guilty.

From this guilt arises the necessity for the poem itself. It has after all a religious position, and put in religious terms its function is to praise, not to explain or controvert. In the hierarchy of doxology it occupies a higher position than prayer, for though prayer, being a private conversation with the Absolute, is by this fact situated in a higher category of action—it is a consummate act of communication—the poem fulfils its function by transforming our relation to reality by an act of thaumaturgy. Within the Just City which is the poem even our guilt becomes an object of praise: O felix Culpa.

Leaving aside those curious things which people are always asking of art, of the poem—how to treat their wives, escape boredom, vote at the next election etc.—there is this overriding character of all poetry, that it affirms, glorifies, praises.

It is in the light of this fact that the morality of Barker's poetry must be viewed, for few poets have shown a clearer and more constant awareness of this central aspect of the activity than he has.

III

The effect on the psychology of the ethical directive, and the effect of the pure act of praise that undertakes no instruction, are sufficiently similar for a confusion to arise. A certain exhilaration of spirit that comes from the illusion that one has been raised above the condition of utter indecision is common to each experience. The normal condition of man being one of confusion and amorphous unease.

Moral certitude, which is the basis of vision in art, as in philosophy, is the most compelling of qualities. In the case of the poet we have to face the fact that this certitude can exist without a clear structure of belief in the philosophical sense. At the same time, it is this quality of transcendent affirmation of all things that exist, and, as Barker insists, of those whose existence is unknown to us, that forms the essence of poetic excitement.

Again we must acknowledge the fact that the poet operates in a world of paradox. For Barker, for instance, the most exhilarating act of the arrogant imagination was the Greek shrine to the unknown god. An act at once of humility and spiritual arrogance.

One is involved in obscure matters when one raises the position of human uncertainty, human despair even, in the scale of great moral certainties that constitute the poem. But this very concern has been conspicuously Barker's. There is Keats' famous sentence which he has quoted in his essay on Shakespeare when speaking of these things:

At once it struck me what quality went to form a man of achievement, especially in literature, and which Shakespeare possessed so enormously—I mean Negative Capability, that is when a man is capable of being in uncertainties, mysteries, doubts without any irritable reaching after fact and reason.

The kind of affirmation that the poem seeks to make does not belong to the order of fact or reason, though its message, if such must be asked for, is rejoicing in reality and acceptance of life. For Matthew Arnold poetry was a criticism of life, and Barker started from a position where he accepts this view: but in the evolution of his thought over twenty years he moves further into the Dionysian world where poetry occupies a different relation to religion,* a nearer relation to the void.

> The poem affirms spiritually what it cannot possibly declare intellectually. Every poem is thus a making known of ourselves to the Unknown God.

Or again:

> The void gibbers. What ensues for us takes on the appearance of a revelation or an inspiration. The voice of the unknowable has spoken out of a cloud of unknowing.

Barker has placed himself in a special relation to the abyss at whose edge we all live whether we acknowledge it or not.

But the first poet to open up deliberately this unknown territory, as Pierre Jean Jouve has remarked, was Charles Baudelaire. Two things run through the work of Barker which demonstrate his relationship to Baudelaire: his vision of evil and his sense of the Void.

These things are analagous but not identical. Baudelaire's *Le Gouffre* is a profound and universal fact of all our psychology, and Barker's gibbering void is another manifestation of it. But with the characteristic difference that he has discarded the devious satanic approach. Their common ground may well be simply Augustinian Christianity.

IV

The poetry of Baudelaire is more relevant for us than ever to-day.

* 'Poetry is not a criticism of life. Religion is a criticism of life.'

This may be a commonplace. Pierre Jean Jouve, in a beautiful as well as important essay on Baudelaire, has made the case.

What is interesting is the fact that the terms of reference in this essay have little relation to any recent English poet with the possible exception of George Barker.

The following may be stated as at least a useful approximation to the truth: Laforgue was right in his enumeration of the points of originality in Baudelaire. Eliot and Pound made use of certain aspects of Baudelaire's vision via Laforgue. But there remained an area uncharted even by Laforgue, an area of religious vision of evil, and of that remote but vital 'source inconsciente de la poesie' that has not, even yet, produced its most profound effects or yielded its full riches.

For this must be said: that while Baudelaire was indeed the first (as Laforgue remarked) to speak in the subdued tones of the confessional, to speak as an ordinary lost soul, who is not triumphant but accuses himself, he is also the first to endow poetry with a kind of importance that freed it from the notions of entertainment and communication.*

Laforgue saw that Baudelaire had made poetry 'something for the initiated'. . . . 'I am condemned on account of the public—good—the public is not admitted.' But the basis of this view lay in the new relationship to reality that Baudelaire had arrived at through his art, a vision of evil at the heart of all action . . . 'Nous sommes tous nés marques pour le mal' and the acknowledgement of *Le Gouffre*. Jouve puts it: 'Baudelaire, après Dante, figure le plus grand poete ayant le sens du pêché, non pas formellement selon la casuistique, mais essentiallement et dans la fonction de vivre.'

> La sottise l'erreur le pêché la lesine
> Occupent nos esprit et travaillent nos corps.

* A more private and mysterious idea of poetry in fact: 'starting with his direct descendants Mallarmé and Rimbaud poetry had to write silences, note the inexpressible'
—Pierre Jean Jouve, *Tombeau de Baudelaire*

And also:

> most of the errors relating to the Beautiful are the result of
> the false conception of morality which prevailed during the
> 18th century. . . . The denial of the dogma of original sin
> played no small part in the blindness of the age.

I am not going to suggest that Barker's position is identical
with that of Baudelaire, even in relation to his view of evil.
What is true is that he bears a relationship to these ideas that
places him in a very different historical perspective from any
other contemporary English poet.

I have not chosen to attempt to place the psychological
position of these ideas in relation to Barker's verse. Partly
because of disgust with too much psychology, and partly
because they derive from a region not easily accessible to
psychology—the region of Baudelaire's 'homme spirituel',
where words like soul and sin must still be invoked. Nevertheless, the personal anguish of the poet inhabits these poems;
dominates their ritualistic formal existence.

To comment on it one needs to raise a question of some
importance: the position of the Mask in the work of Barker.

> Leaning in the evenings, I live
> Between a dream and a mask
> The dogs of memory, howling, shall
> Mourn on the steps of the heart.
>
> Lost in the temporal labyrinth
> How shall I find that exit?
> O follow backward the fallen face and
>   the fragments
> Of desecrated existence!

V

It will not be surprising if reflection on the work of a poet who believes that . . . 'the image exercises its profundity in proportion to the number of strata or masks it wears to conceal, and at the same time to characterize, the profundities in which it exists' . . . reveals that the Mask plays a role of some importance both in his imagery and in his attitudes.

By the Mask I do not mean merely that which hides its essential character or origins in an appearance that is somehow contrary to its true nature. I do not mean merely perversity. There is that too, but also there is the ritual, the personal rite. And there is this as an instrument for excavation in territory too terrifying for direct vision, for direct statement.

The mind of the artist is commonly haunted by a dream of direct contact (and from that direct statement) with the very nexus of his vision.

The last great poet to fall under this supreme temptation ended a trader in the colonies, and died writing a demand note for an imaginary debt to a nonexistent debtor. This remark is less than serious in that it does not to a degree take into account the dreadful suffering preceding the eve of the death on which this letter was written. Nevertheless, it is a fact that Rimbaud made the impossible attempt, and consequences did follow. For we do not know what happens to those who frontally assault the mystery, what they see they cannot tell, and who knows what they feel since there is no vehicle of communication, no evidence at all.

Thus the mask is what allows a man to penetrate in deep regions of the mind and soul and yet survive, not to disappear forever.

If it were possible to penetrate into the ultimate regions where the poem has its most profound existence then he who so penetrated would do precisely this, disappear. This is how I interpret Barker's introductory lines to his collected poems:

'And what, said the Emperor, does this poem describe?'
'It describes,' said the Poet, 'the Cave of the Never-Never.
Would you like to see what's inside?' He offered his arm.
They stepped into the poem and disappeared forever.

These verses should have forwarned those reviewers of Barker's
poems who approached the task armed with the principles of
the anti-romanticism of the early part of this century. We are
still overshadowed by the prodigious task performed by Pound
and Eliot, the strictures and prejudices arising from it have
been invoked in derogation of Barker. For such criticisms his
work presents an easy enough target. Nevertheless, it is best to
leave these objections behind when we enter the world of
Barker's consciousness. For here in a region of religious pressure, where the wounded eros cries out for liberation from the
mesh of a guilt-ridden subconscious, a region of old escha-
tological thought and even older instincts towards immolation,
these objections lose much of their usefulness. For the rhetoric
is not the vague dressing up of unimportant doubtful attitudes
to look like poetic experience, it is the result of attempting to
speak of the unspeakable. And, as Kierkegaard has it, when
being diverted by experiments in natural magic there is nothing more odious than to have an obstinate fellow along who is
incredulous about everything although he is never able to
explain the tricks.

The use of the terms 'Poet' and 'Emperor' and the 'Cave of
the Never-Never' and the gentle air of allegory and fable intro-
duces us to one aspect of the mask the Barkerian vision wears.
There is the characteristic lightness of touch, which although
abandoned on necessary occasions is never wholly beyond his
command, but which does not disguise the serious fact that
Barker writes always as Poet, dedicated and possessed, trapped
certainly in the biological cage, but speaking from that far
world of ultimate mysteries.

Here then is one Mask. Unexpectedly that of THE POET.

68

The poem then becomes a formal rite, and in keeping with this we find a severe and at times maniacal attention to form. A love of the riddle, the pun, the inversion. I do not feel that this requires demonstration. It is borne in on one even by a superficial reading of the verse. A superficial reading of the verse leaves us still at the level of this Mask and not yet hearing the strange undertones of the anguished human.

But this Mask needs a respectable genealogy in order to fulfil the role it is called on to play. For the poet, having set his feet on this particular road, is there as much a victim of the laws of act and consequence as he is in any other sphere, and becomes in turn the victim of the mask. A certain courage is needed to preserve the consistency which alone will then save him, as poet.

Barker is however a Catholic in another sense: he is a Catholic by the simple fact of birth and education. And the Mask here has two distinguished forebears. Firstly Baudelaire; but the second overriding and original instigator: Saint Augustine. It relies for its usefulness on the Augustinian Christian concept of *PERSONALITY*. It should be observed that the word is latin and differs essentially from the Greek 'character'. What it has to do with is the notion of the activity of the Logos and of its situation.

VI

The Mask hides the personal suffering.

The raw material of the poems, the occasions of moral distress, the minutiæ of defeat and humiliation are not made known. These have been apotheosised into the poem and are contained in it. To such an extent that certain poems of Barker's, that wear the mask of simple poetic invocations, can be read as biographic detail, given the key. The key is not given, we discover it occasionally and by accident, but the poetry in its innate character bears no relation to the confession. Or if any relation a very devious one. The events, the facts of the poet's experience, are given back in the heightened language of the imagination, transposed on to another plane and set in a new moral relationship. They have been transmogrified in their passage through the Personality of the poet.

The imagination is the active agent of this transmogrification. For there is on the one hand that form of expression which is palpably no more than a cry of human anguish— nearly all Celtic (I mean Gaelic) poetry comes within this category, and is not poetry of a high order for this reason—and there is the detached enunciation of the moral realities of a situation, of which Dante perhaps provides the supreme example.

There are two elements involved: there is the poet suffering the horror of being human—the disgusting facts of existence— and there is the human cursed by the affliction of harbouring the moral maniac who is the poet. This irreconcilable marriage can only find harmony in the poem. The authority for this blessing comes from the voice of the Logos, wherein the poet finds his moral imperative. The activity of the Logos in the creature constitutes the essence of *PERSONALITY*.

Per sonare—to sound through: in its very elements the concept of personality is anti-objective anti-scientific. For the detachment of the poet must not be confused with the so-called objectivity of the scientist. The 'scientific approach', and its concomitant ideology are the inventions of the Greeks. They held total sway in the classical world until displaced by Christianity. Intellectually, until displaced by the Trinitarianism of Saint Augustine.* For Augustine the concept of personality was part of a new and effective technique of salvation.

The essence of this technique lay in the first place in freeing

* For a proper exposition of the nature and historical position of this I refer the reader to C. N. Cochrane's *Christianity and Classical Culture*.

the mind from the ignorance and myopia that resulted from a misunderstanding of the possibilities of the instrument of apprehension. Emancipation from 'ignorantia' and 'caecitas'.

In accepting the scientific view, man was committing himself to a distorted and incomplete picture of reality. Emancipated from this misuse of the faculty of apprehension, he could perceive that the divisions of Form and Matter were nothing more than abstractions of his own fancy; could recognise that there was an alternative to the Platonic disembodied impersonal One and to the sad condemnation to a purely quantitative world; could begin to perceive the existence and activity of the Logos within his own breast. For Augustine, the scientific view, the rational objectivity of classic thought and theology, represented a misuse of the faculties of the creature. But the roots of this misuse, of this obsession with science and of the further obsessions of science, lay not in the intellect of man but in the affections.

Thus Augustine sees the philosophic problem as really a moral dilemma. He sees in the obsession with the objectifying detachment of science an egotistic passion for independence. An adherence to the delusion of self sufficiency. Where this morality leads Saint Augustine himself in relation to art is an interesting matter but not relevant here.

From the point of view of Barker's work it is the profound basis that this attitude offers for a personal subjectivity that matters.

I have now strayed into the realms of true religion. This is unavoidable. I doubt if it is possible to discuss Barker's work at all seriously without penetrating to some extent into the world of religious belief. He himself asserts the supreme importance of religion. For him poetry cannot usurp the responsibilities of religion. The poet cannot operate without the sanction of the religious man, whereas the religious man can pray without reference to the poet. The category of prayer being of a higher order than that of the poem.

71

The subjectivity that the concept of personality brought into being also meant a new sort of responsibility. It is part of a technique of salvation, and thus alters man's relation to event and time. The fact of the Logos and its activity within the creature endows man with an uniqueness different from that of classic thought, creates for him a different relationship with the mystery, the numen, God.

The mystery is active within him, and his fate is to that extent in his own hands. He is not fixed in his fate but capable of transforming his position by his own choices, by paying attention to the voices within. Because of the relation of the poet to the spiritual man this has profound significance in poetry.

It must not however be assumed, as this necessarily crude glance at the history of these ideas might suggest, that the innovations of Christian thought present a total historical break, profound and far reaching as they are. The techniques of classic philosophy, though predisposed to the objectifying detachment of science, were nevertheless turned towards ultimate reality, and still able to encounter the deepest mystery with reverence. Unlike certain modern atheistic philosophies.

For no matter how much the universe seemed to submit to the regimentation of science, man still encountered his world with wonder and awe. Aristotle, for all his method, still postulated the first cause, the unmoved mover.

It is in his comments on the metaphysics of Aristotle that the sentence of Aquinas occurs: The philosopher is related to the poet in that both are concerned with *mirandum*. This strikes me as a serious remark and one relevant to the moment. For confessional disclosures about aspects of the individual psychology do not constitute a considerable substitute for the mirandum of which Saint Thomas Aquinas speaks. There is the Mystery, and it will always be the important part of the poet's function to acknowledge it; and unless science can explain origins (and not merely origin of species but the origin of

72

our existence and its purpose) it will remain unsatisfying to the serious mind.

Evaluation is not a function of reason: reason deals with accepted facts, including accepted values. Ignorance of this is the root of rational philistinism.

For Barker, the realities of the poem are essentially of a non-objective non-rational order. This being true, of course, of the Greek poem, as of all poetry. For I have been referring to the history of ideas, ideas which affect the poet but cannot alter the essence of poetry. The essential poetic ability has been stated by Barker many years ago thus:

> The exploitation, by the imagination, or process of poetry, of the sensual world, of events and persons, in such a manner that an intuitive rather than a rational evaluation of them is achieved—I take this to be the highest and the best ability of the poet; and perhaps, indeed the only true poetic ability of which he is capable.

VII

Viewed in the light of the Mask many of the difficulties presented by Barker's rhetoric disappear.

What appears to be verbalism has meaning. Provided we remember the relationship to reality postulated by Barker's concept of THE POET.

In the first place the heightened language represents the real or actual world of event and fact as it is apotheosised into the poem. It is at the same time a description of event and a transposition of event onto a higher moral plane. In this way the religious man in Barker is satisfied by the poet in him, and the suffering human is also expressed. The mask of the poet contains the reality of the human and the reality of the religious man. Its meaning proceeds in deepening layers, the key to which lies in the moral needs of the reader. Just as its origin lies in the moral needs of the poet.

Barker's poems, although they wear a formal, ritual, and rhetorical dress for the most part, are in fact as full of things as an old lumber room. If we cannot off-hand recognise the old shoe that pinched, it is merely because the poet has polished it up somewhat, but it is nonetheless the old shoe. Serving also now, however, its mysterious double, treble, god knows what stint, in the new service to which it has been conscripted. And this special kind of responsibility to the real world is something which Barker constantly honours. His poems do not contain lies in that they are true to the conditions of their own existence. This existence is not conditioned by the idea of communication, or instruction, or social usefulness. For Barker, the only possible vehicle of communication is love, not words, and 'if a little love gets through/ Then we are luckier than most'. But in fact he offers no anodyne to the truth that we are each one irrevocably doomed to aloneness; and art for him is, as Samuel Beckett has it, the apotheosis of solitude. Beckett's analysis of this condition of the poet's existence fairly describes Barker's position and is worth quotation:

> . . . the only possible spiritual development is in the sense of depth. The artistic tendency is not expansive but a contraction. And art is the apotheosis of solitude. There is no communication because there are no vehicles of communication. Even on the rare occasions when word and gesture happen to be valid expressions of the personality, they lose their significance on their passage through the cataract of the personality that is opposed to them. Either we speak and act for ourselves in which case speech and action are distorted and emptied of their meaning by an intelligence that is not ours or else we speak and act for others—in which case we speak and act a lie.

What then is the answer to this condition? For the poet, Ezra Pound's explanation or statement of how the poem gets written explains his immediate relationship to the dilemma:

74

They were made for no man's entertainment but because a man *believing in silence* found himself unable to withhold from speaking.

In the work of Barker I see a deeply religious nature break silence in anguish. And the anguish has its roots in the internecine embrace of eros and the spiritual man in the person of the poet.

Two Poems

for George Barker

OLIVER BERNARD

1

afternoon sunshine a fine rain of hair
queen snip behind me kneels the summer air
plays round her bare waist and my ticklish shoulders

cool elbows hover angels round my head
she lily gilds me with slim whispering steel
ice cream has nothing on the smile I feel

half naked aping samson on the grass
I lay aside my jawbone of an ass
the philistines stroll unmolested by

castration complex permanently waived
having it cut off's painless in such weather
pleasant if you can get it done by heather

2

good friday cars drew up and stared
across the liver coloured water
some of their drivers seemed prepared
to stay till dusk somebody's daughter
twisted the mirror tangle haired

these went who came some angels made
cups of tea and contemplated
northwest skies fresh winds obeyed
necessities and agitated
reeds and waves while children played

only the clocks were busy this
wasted afternoon the sun
dazzled the gravel where the kiss
of cloudy wavelets made all run
glistening in non human bliss

A Few Memories: In Homage

ANTHONY THWAITE

Between the ages of fifteen and seventeen, I seem to have composed several letters of homage and/or sheer impertinence to living poets who had momentarily taken my fancy. I wrote to T. S. Eliot concerning my doubts about Christianity: he did not reply. I wrote to C. Day Lewis to confirm my conviction that the way of Dylan Thomas was the only hope for poetry: he replied courteously and charmingly, and I now wonder why I didn't have the cheek to write to Thomas himself. I wrote to Henry Treece, enclosing a critical essay on his work, on which he commented that he was grateful for the flattering things I had said but preferred old English sheepdogs to poets.

But these letters and the opinions they carried were only sudden impulses. My true homage was to George Barker. I suppose I must have first read his poems in Michael Roberts's *Faber Book of Modern Verse* and Yeats's Oxford anthology, but I know that the first book of his I bought was *Calami-terror*, in a Birmingham bookshop visited when changing trains on the way back to boarding school in Bath. I was sixteen. Immediately I knew that my pantheon of Langland, Blake and Dylan Thomas would have to be extended. For a long time after that it was a bad week if I hadn't written six poems, and all of them rolled and reverberated with Barkerian rhetoric.

Being the school poet was a heady but frustrating job. I was steered away from my ambition to edit the school literary magazine, *Piazza*, by schoolmasters who averred that it would interfere with my Latin, though I still think the real reason was they supposed it would make me more swollen-headed than I was already. The next best thing was to contribute copiously to the magazine, which I did. My efforts included a poem called 'Variation on a Theme by George Barker', which took a line from *Calamiterror* and descanted on it. When *Piazza* was printed, I slipped a copy of it into an envelope, along with sundry other poems of mine, and sent it to this unknown but hallowed George Barker c/o Faber & Faber.

The response was all I could have hoped. A thin foreign-feeling envelope arrived from the south of France, addressed to me in spiky Elizabethan handwriting. Mr Barker liked my poem; he advised me to keep my singing robes well laundered; to my absurd question, 'Am I a poet, do you think I am any good?' he opined that it was really a matter of 'For God's sake stop or for God's sake go on'; and that he supposed I was young. He also wrote that, since my Muse appeared to have more mandrake than man in her, he suggested I use blood.

I thirsted for such assurances, such apopthegms. A few loyal friends were shown the letter, and were impressed, and before long I had packed up an even larger envelope and sent its load of verses to George Barker. This time the reply came from London. It confirmed the earlier remarks about being a poet, and went on to say: 'The poet is a scapegoat disguised as a scrapegrace. See to it that you acquire the grace to escape from'. Most head-turning of all, the letter ended: 'If you are ever in London, why not come and break salt with me or whatever the hell it is one breaks'.

My inclination was to leap on the next London train and make straight for Stanhope Gardens, S.W.7. But it was term time, Somerset was a long way from London, and in any case I spent the holidays in Leicester with my parents. I hardly knew London at all, and couldn't imagine when I might go there.

But then, fortuitously, my father's job was moved to Muswell Hill: the literary mysteries of the capital were about to be revealed to me. The next holidays—of Christmas 1947—I arrived in South Kensington with an A-Z street-guide and presented myself at the Barker doorstep.

He was not there; he was round the corner mending a car with his brother Kit. So my first view of the legendary poet was of a well-sculpted but greased face peering out from under the chassis of a large, battered but powerful vehicle. I announced myself. 'At last', he said, and as far as I was concerned all became a blur. I remember little of whatever else happened that afternoon, except that I think we visited an exhibition at the Victoria & Albert. But he looked and sounded and behaved exactly as a poet should.

And that was and is his importance to me, quite apart from the value of the poetry itself. During the eighteen months or so that followed, I saw George Barker a few times: I remember one meeting in particular, in the Black Horse in Rathbone Place, just off Oxford Street, when I drank an unaccustomed quantity of bitter and heard him speak the astounding words, 'I'll show your poems to Eliot, if you like, and see whether he wants them for Faber'. Whether the offer was ever taken up, and, if it was, what Eliot thought of them, I don't know. But the kindness, the amused seriousness, the refusal to reduce this naïve, pert, opinionated, baby-faced public schoolboy to pulp (which he could so easily have done) have always stayed with me. Later, when I left school and had to do my army service, I wrote to George Barker from Winchester and Bodmin and various garrisons in Libya, and had from him some well-chosen mantic epigrams and advice (such as that, if I were going to hand-print a booklet of my poems—an idea that came to nothing—I should somehow acquire a font of Bodoni, because it had the proper shape for poems). Some of the letters were written in that characteristic hand, others were typed with generous triple-spacing onto a brown ribbon I have never

80

seen anywhere else. They all had what someone has called *une nature riche.*

He came to Oxford when I was an undergraduate there, and at my invitation read his poems to the university poetry society, drinking with only a few aspersions the foul British-type sherry we provided and swaying down my spiral stair-case with the remark, 'My dear Thwaite, you cost too much'. After Oxford, my wife and I visited him on our honeymoon, slopping down a muddy cart-track somewhere near Haslemere and finding him in a woodcutter's cottage with no running water. We were about to sail for Japan, where I was to take up my first job teaching at Tokyo University. Of his own experiences at Sendai in 1940, he told us that he was followed everywhere by a tiny spy in white gloves, and that the calligraphy was upsetting. This was challenging, though I discovered that my own feelings were different about 'the island where/The soul is shallower than a bowl of tea/And negative as water'. But of course he was there at a particularly bad time.

There have been long periods between 1947 and today when I haven't been in touch with George Barker, haven't even known whether he was in Italy or Islington, Norfolk or Nevada. But he has been a presence, a type, an example at the back of my consciousness of what a poet's calling is. As a radio producer and editor, I broadcast and published him, but always with the suspicion that the true poet is not a go-between or cultural functionary. I suppose that what I am saying is that I still have Romantic aspirations towards some imagined ideal of the poet—aspirations that may seem belied by the kind of poetry I have written myself and the kind of professional life I have led; and that such an ideal is embodied in George Barker.

I have suddenly realized that I am now eight years older than George Barker was when, in my guise of what he once called 'AngelThwace', I first met him under that car in South Kensington. It's a chastening thought. To have achieved what he has done in the best of his poems, without compromises and solely devoted to his art, is an example to the less single-minded of us. He will continue to be an example, long after the age of sixty.

For the Sixtieth Birthday of
George Barker

C. H. SISSON

My first encounter with the work of George Barker must have been in March 1933, the date of *New Verse*, No. 2. In that number there appeared a poem—not in the collected edition—called *Coward's Song*. Barker was then twenty. I was nineteen, an undergraduate reading Philosophy and English Literature in a university which owed its existence largely to a firm the products of which were still some years from having been declared carcinogenic. The sham gothic was in such beautiful stone that you could not call that university red-brick, even if that subjective classification had by then been invented, which it had not. This academy was provincial, a term which is exact and not shameful, so far as I can see. There were some disadvantages about it, as compared with Oxford and Cambridge which were supposed to be the only proper universities, but they cannot have included any great obstruction to the diffusion of the most interesting literature of the day. For at nineteen, and without assistance from any initiatives but my own, I was already acquainted with the work not only of Eliot, Pound and Joyce but that of Auden and even Clere Parsons. I had become a reader of *New Verse* with the first number in January, 1933.

I have sometimes wondered, since, at this rapid diffusion of novelty. It was not due to any activity on the part of our accredited teachers, for whom Eliot was still unacademic. Eliot and Joyce had been presented to me, before I left school, by a smug reader of an earlier generation, Harold Nicolson, in a series of broadcast talks. The diffusion of Auden, Spender and Day Lewis took advantage of the political currents of the time. I think our knowledge of what was going on, in this field, and the fact that we were less cut off than we might have been, must have owed a good deal to people who cared more for politics than they did for literature and in particular to those who, with the hermetic advantages of Party Members, circulated more freely among their fellow-conspirators in Oxford, Cambridge and London than anyone would have bothered to do—or could have afforded—in search merely of the latest literary enthusiasms of undergraduates. It was rather immoral not to be a Communist, and 1933 was the year when Hitler came to power.

All this was far from the reality of politics, if there can be said to be such a thing, but young people are apt to believe violently in the present—and how right, from a certain point of view, they are—and by a heady projection in the immediate future, which always turns out to be different. With all this passion the *Coward's Song* had nothing to do. The characteristic lucidity of the time—or what was reckoned as such—was in such verses as those of Auden in *New Verse* No. 1:

> I have a handsome profile
> I've been to a great public school
> I've a little money invested
> Then why do I feel such a fool
> As if I owned a world that had had its day?

The tone of George Barker's poem was different, and the indications it gave were different:

> From nineteen pointed star
> Roll into dull stone

84

The soul lying on the seashore,
Even by the ubiquitous sea unnoticed
And ignored.

Geoffrey Grigson, who edited *New Verse*, was far from being a
victim of the juvenile politics of the moment. If his periodical
was carried by this movement of sentiment into corners it
would not otherwise have penetrated, his own objectives were
more serious. 'Poets in this country and during this period of
the victory of the masses, aristocratic and bourgeois as much
as proletarian,' he said in the explanatory note prefixed to
No 1, 'which have captured the instruments of access to the
public and use them to convey their own timid and silent
vulgarity, vulgarising all the arts, are allowed no longer
periodical means of communicating their poems.' His object
was to provide such a means, 'for sixpence—the price of ten
Players or a brief library borrowing of *Angel Pavement* or a
'bus fare from Piccadilly Circus to Golders Green.' Far-off
prices! And it is not only the currency, but the 'instruments of
access to the public', which have become incomparably more
debased since that time. It is a measure of Grigson's ability as
an editor that he did not allow himself to be swept even on the
sentimental current of his superior readers. In No 2 he was
already saying that it was 'stupid to keep in fancy these three'
—*the* three, Spender, Auden and Day Lewis—'as triune. The
three are distinct.' He went on, in his review of Day Lewis's
The Magnetic Mountain—published significantly by the
Hogarth Press which was still working for the supremacy of
Bloomsbury—to put his finger on the crucial weaknesses of the
future poet laureate and laurel-bearer of the Arts Council—if
one may speak that much ill of the dead. And while the selec-
tion of poems for publication naturally gave prominence to the
Communist orientation of several of the best poets, which was
a matter of fact, place was given equally, when the quality of
the verse was held to deserve it, to those who were not left

85

wing or not left wing in the manner which was generally thought obligatory. The contributors included even Allen Tate and that odd man out David Gascoyne, then a surrealist. It was this catholicity which gave first place in No 2 to the *Coward's Song* of George Barker.

The next two or three years—a long time when one is around twenty—took me to a Germany over-run by Storm Troopers and a Paris torn by the agitations preceding the advent of the Front populaire. Certainly my political scepticism was not thereby diminished. After that I was in London and had found a niche in Whitehall for which, as one of my Oxford-bred university teachers had prophetically told me, my background was unsuitable. I had accidentally heard the clatter of hooves and stood by while the heralds proclaimed King George VI to a deserted square, just by the statue of Charles I. With everybody else I had lived through the phantom-haunted days of Bad Godesberg and Munich in which a civil servant, Sir Horace Wilson, distinguished himself so abjectly. It was then, at a time when my mind was filled by prominent public events, that I came upon Barker's work again. I must be slow for I have noticed that it has sometimes taken me several years to receive the impact of a new writer. The pre-conceptions one has, at any particular time, about what poetry should be like, count for something in this. I remember how, as a sixth-former of sixteen, I had been awed by the *Songs of Innocence and Experience* without really taking Blake into the canon, he was so different. The work of Barker's I now came across was the *Elegies Number One and Two*, published as the opening of the New Series of *New Verse*, in January 1939. The poems buzzed with a romanticism I did not wholly admit of. At the same time they uncovered imaginative depths the reality of which could not be denied. The novelty was that this extreme subjectivism came nearer to mirroring the shocking events of the time than all the patter on matters of current interest, whether in verse or in newspapers:

The tragedy is Time foreshadowing its climax.
Thus in the stage of time the minor moth is small
But prophesies the Fokker with marvellous wings
Mottled with my sun's gold and your son's blood.

It is easy to recognise the picture after the event, and no doubt
the Apocalypse which took place in Soho while people like
myself were passing a life of servitude overseas tended to
overdo the splendours so that the words became detached
from the realities.

Barker might easily have petered out among the romanti-
cisms of the forties. But a poet who is not dead develops, and
his best work was to come after the war. It is to the permanent
shame of the publishers of the *Collected Poems 1930–1955* that
they would not admit to that volume *The True Confession of
George Barker*, 'which Mr Barker wished to include', as a foot-
note to the table of contents explains. It was to date and probably remains his best poem. The romanticism was suddenly
combined with a new and matter-of-fact tone. The poem is
obscene, as it was still possible to be in 1950, when it was first
published in a little pamphlet by Fore Publications Limited.
It could also be reckoned blasphemous, if there is anyone
around who still reckons in such terms. Barker no doubt
wished it to be both, and he was successful. Such success in
registering the contents of their minds is given to few people,
and a poet is one who is successful. A lot of living goes to the
making of a few pages of verse. In this poem, with a quite new
lucidity, Barker came up with his results. One cannot understand the motives of a publisher who wishes us to ignore them.
When I first met Barker, corralled by David Wright at last in
the bar of the Red Lion in Duke of York Street, just across the
road from my office in St. James's Square, I realised that I was
in the presence of a profound humourist.

This is not a guide to the works of George Barker. It is the
side-long personal impact of one of the most remarkable figures

of the age, who is only a year away from being a precise contemporary, that I am trying to define. And I cannot say with
what pleasure I received, inscribed with New Year wishes for
the year 1970, a copy of the beautifully produced little volume,
At Thurgarton Church. For what a poet most needs to do is to
go on, and in these hundred and fifty lines, more or less,
Barker had once more found a new tone. It was grave and
collected his experience afresh from the angle to which the
further years had brought him.

> And there in the livid dust
> and bones of death we search
> until we find as we must
> outside Thurgarton Church
> only wild grasses blow.

*Non est sanitas in carne mea a facie irae tuae: non est pax ossibus
meis, a facie peccatorum meorum.* 'There is no health in my
flesh because of thy displeasure: neither is there any rest in my
bones, by reason of my sin.' This is from the Psalter. 'We die in
the clay we dread', Barker's poem says. I cannot express my
regard for him more, on his sixtieth birthday, than by saying
that I think his seventieth will be an occasion for celebrating
the work he will have done in the next ten years; that it will be
appropriate and characteristic work; and that further than
that I have no idea what its shape or content will be.

Bibliography

Works by George Barker

Alanna Autumnal. Wishart: London, 1933. 87pp.

Thirty Preliminary Poems. David Archer: London, 1933. 37pp.

Janus (The Documents of a Death—The Bacchant. Two Tales). Faber & Faber: London, 1935. 301pp.

Poems. Faber & Faber: London, 1935. 64pp.

Calamiterror. Faber & Faber: London, 1937. 53pp.

Elegy on Spain. Manchester Contemporary Bookshop, 1939. Illustrated, 10pp.

Lament and Triumph. Faber & Faber: London, 1940. 78pp.

Selected Poems. Macmillan & Co. New York, 1941.

Sacred and Secular Elegies. New Directions: Norfolk, Conn., 1943.

Eros in Dogma. Faber & Faber: London, 1944. 61pp.

Love Poems. Dial Press: New York, 1947. 79pp.

The Dead Seagull. John Lehmann: London, 1950. 142pp.

—(Farrar, Strauss & Young: New York, 1951).

—(MacGibbon & Kee: London, 1965. 111pp).

News of the World. Faber & Faber: London, 1950. 64pp.

The True Confession of George Barker. Fore Publications: London, 1950. 36pp.

—(Parton Press: London, 1957. 50 copies signed by the author).

—(With the addition of Part II. MacGibbon & Kee: London, 1965. 86pp).

A Vision of Beasts and Gods. Faber & Faber: London, 1954. 62pp.

Collected Poems, 1930–1955. Faber & Faber: London, 1957. 245pp.

Two Plays (The Seraphina. In the Shade of the Old Apple Tree). Faber & Faber: London, 1958. 80pp.

George Barker, Martin Bell, Charles Causley (Selected Poems). Penguin Modern Poets No 3, Penguin; 1962.

The View From a Blind I. Faber & Faber: London, 1962.

Dreams of a Summer Night. Faber & Faber: London, 1966. 71pp.

At Thurgarton Church. Trigram Press: London, 1969. Illustrated, 26pp.

To Aylsham Fair. Faber & Faber: London, 1970. Illustrated, 78pp.

Essays. MacGibbon & Kee: London, 1970. 191pp.

Poems of Places and People. Faber & Faber: London, 1971.

The Alphabetical Zoo. Faber & Faber: London, 1972.

Selected Articles and Reviews by George Barker

Adelphi IV, June 1932: Review of *New Signatures*, and *New Bearings in English Poetry*.

Criterion XI 426–429, July 1932: *Letters of Robert Burns* ed. by J. de Lancey Ferguson.

Criterion XIII, 426–429, April 1934: Daedalus (poem).

Criterion XIV, 649, July 1935: Ezra Pound: *A Draft of Cantos XXXI–XLI*.

Criterion XV, 440, April 1936: Winter Idyll (poem).

Criterion, XVI, 33–37, October 1936: Ode to Man, Part 1 (poem).

New Verse XXVI–XXVII, November 1937: '16 Comments on Auden'.

Purpose X, Jan-March 1938: 'A Note on the Dialectics of Poetry'.

Criterion XVII, 583, April 1938: *Quia Amore Leugues* ed. by H. S. Bennett; and, *The Cherry and the Sloe* by Alexander Montgomerie, ed. by H. Harvey Wood.

Criterion XVIII, 54–66, Jan 1939: Poetry and Reality.

Life and Letters Today XXIII, Oct 1939: 'Funeral Eulogy for Garcia Lorca'.

New Poems, 1940 (ed. Oscar Williams) Foreword: 'All Poems are Elegies'. The Yardstick Press, New York, 1941.

Nation, CLIII, 1941: 'When Greek Meets English', Review of

Oedipus at Colonnus by Sophocles, an English version by Robert Fitzgerald.

— 'Three Tenant Families', Review of *Let Us Now Praise Famous Men* by James Agee and Walker Evans.

— 'Huxley as Theologian', Review of *Grey Eminence: A Study in Religion and Politics*, by Aldous Huxley.

New Republic, Oct 1941: 'The Chameleon Poet', Review of *Rainer Maria Rilke* by E. M. Butler.

Nation, CLVII, Nov 1941: Review of *The Beautiful People* by William Saroyan.

New Republic, CV, Dec 1941: 'Notes From the Largest Imaginary Empire'.

Nation, CLIII, Dec 1941: 'Poe as Symbol', Review of *Edgar Alan Poe: A Critical Biography* by Arthur Hobson Quinn.

Nation, CLIV, Jan 1942: 'Henry Miller, Rivivalist', Review of *The Colossus of Maroussi* by Henry Miller.

Nation, CLIV, Feb 1942: 'James Joyce, Heretic', Review of *James Joyce* by Harry Levin.

— 'Mr Jolas', Review of *Verticle* ed. Eugene Jolas.

Nation, CLIV, April 1942: 'In All Directions', Review of *New Directions in Prose and Poetry*, 1941, ed. James Laughlin.

—'A Study of Robert Bridges', Review of *Robert Bridges: A Study of Traditionalism in Poetry* by Albert Guerard.

New Republic CVI, April 1942: 'A Spray for the Nightingale', Review of *Awake! And Other Wartime Poems* by W. R. Rodgers.

The New Yorker, XVIII; July–Oct 1942: 'Improbable Empire'.

Poetry London, No 13, June–July 1948: 'The Fat Lady at the Circus'.

Life and Letters Today, LX, Feb 1949: 'A Note on Andre Gide'.

Life and Letters Today, LXIV, Feb 1950: 'The Opinion of George Barker on Some Modern Verse'.

New Statesman & Nation XL, July 1950: 'Poet as Pariah'.

Partisan Review XX, July 1953: 'William Shakespeare and the

Horse with Wings' (Text of a lecture delivered on Shakespeare's birthday at Stratford-on-Avon).

Nimbus, Vol. 2, No 3, Autumn 1954: 'William Shakespeare and the Horse with Wings'.

Encounter II, Jan 1954: 'Dylan Thomas: Memories and Appreciations'.

London Magazine 1, Aug 1954: Review of *The Death Bell* by Vernon Watkins and *The Pot Geranium* by Norman Nicolson.

Nimbus, Vol 3, No 4, 1955: 'Spender and Graham'.

Nimbus, Vol 4, No 3, 1956: 'On the Image'.

London Magazine III, Jan 1956: 'Coming to London'.

Encounter VI, May 1956; 'The Face Behind the Poem: An Essay in Honour of Tennyson' (Reprinted in Poetry XCVII, Feb 1961).

Saturday Review XLIII, Oct 1960: 'The Poem in an Orange Wig'.

Master Poems of the English Language: 'Tennyson's Two Voices', New York, Trident Press, 1966.

The Northern Fiddler: Preface. Brian Higgins, Methuen & Co. Ltd, 1966.

Studies, Comments and Reviews of George Barker

Beecham, Audrey: 'George Barker'. Life and Letters Today, XXV, April–June 1940.

Breit, Harvey: 'View of the World', Poetry LIX, Dec 1941.

Cronin, Anthony: 'Poetry and Ideas: George Barker', London Magazine III, Sept 1956.

Daiches, David: 'The Lyricism of George Barker. Poetry LXIX March 1947.

Day Lewis, Cecil: The Poetic Image. Jonathan Cape, London, 1947.

Fodaski, Martha: Three Memorial Sonnets. Master Poems of the English Language, ed. Oscar Williams, Trident Press, New York, 1966.

— George Barker. Twayne Publishers, New York, 1969.

Friar, Kimon and J. M. Brinnin: 'Myth and Metaphysics', Modern Poetry (An Anthology), New York, 1951.

Golffing, F. C.: 'Mr Barker and his Critics', Review of *Love Poems*, Poetry LXXII, April 1948.

Moore, Geoffrey: 'Wild Words and Personal Symbols', Review of *Collected Poems*.

Potts, Paul: 'The World of George Barker', Poetry Quarterly, Vol 10, No 2, Summer 1956.

Rexroth, Kenneth (ed): The New British Poets: Norfolk, Conn., New Directions.

Scannell, Vernon: 'George Barker: Deep or Drumlie?', The Poetry Review XLV, Oct–Dec 1954.

Scarfe, Francis: 'George Barker: A Pure Poet', *Auden and After*, George Routledge & Sons, 1942.

Sisson, C. H.: 'The Forties', *English Poetry 1900–50*, Rupert Hart-Davis 1971.

Skelton, Robin: 'Allegory of the Adolescent and the Adult', Master Poems of the English Language, Trident Press, New York, 1966.

Swift, Patrick: 'Prolegomenon to George Barker', *x* Vol 1, No 3, June 1960.

Wright, David: 'The Work of George Barker', Nimbus Vol 2, No 3, Autumn 1954.

This edition of *Homage to George Barker* is limited to 275 copies of which 25 copies numbered I–XXV are for private distribution. The remainder are for sale and are numbered 1–250. This copy is number

PRINTER'S COPY